Life is a game called the

'Grand Illusion'

So you may as well

- Look Younger
- Feel Younger
- Be Younger
- Live Longer
- Be Happier

While you learn to play it better.

A Physical, Mental, Emotional and Spiritual approach.

(Zac Simpson-Marvin)

First published October 2014
by Zac Marvin
New Zealand

ISBN 978-0-473-26846-6

This book is not a textbook on physics, chemistry, astronomy, medicine, biology, genetics, psychology, philosophy or any other science. It reflects only an individual world view of the author and his subjective view of some scientific issues and philosophical conceptions. The author's spelling and punctuation are preserved in the text.

Gratitude and Acknowledgement

First and foremost I would like to thank my wife Brigitte for her patience and encouragement in the endeavour of producing this book. Her support was unwavering and positive at all times. I have many friends, to many to mention in fact, that helped in various ways.

Jenny helped so much with my useless spelling and grammar. My other friends helped with ideas and feedback which helped take my original draft to the final result. Friends like Suzanne, Brent, Shane, Lisa, Mike, and many more that hopefully will forgive me for not listing them here.

I would like to thank all the "good" people and situations that have occurred in my life and all the "less than good" people and situations that have occurred in my life as well. It is these that are the real teachers without which I would not be who I am now. Each of them have helped chip away at my ego and have helped me see and bask in the light more clearly.

Lastly thank you dear fellow traveller on the road - may our paths cross in joy, time and time again. Namaste – Zac

Testimonials

What a privilege it was to attend Zac's classes on meditation, spirituality and health. His profound wisdom and knowledge on a vast array of topics is truly amazing. I have been on a spiritual path for over 25 years and yet I still learned much valuable information that I am now incorporating into my own life – to great effect. Zac is highly skilled in imparting his wonderful knowledge in a way that is both easy to understand and enlightening at the same time. I am looking forward to attending more classes in the future.

Karina A, Auckland New Zealand.

Life has a habit of leaping from one thing to another. However, there are some people that make a huge difference along the way. You are one of those people, Zac, and I cherish having met you to experience the absolute abundance of knowledge that you freely give out. Your life's journey has brought such in-depth wisdom, which has been gift-wrapped with your passion and joy. Anyone listening to you will be feeling bright-eyed, inspired and totally focused on every sentence; what I call the "wow!" factor.

I also want to acknowledge that many in our group who, when they first started with you, had none or only a little understanding of how consciousness plays such a major creative role in our life experience. For my friends, you delivered what I hoped you would for them and they now have a consciousness of their own abundance and an understanding that has brought an enthusiastic approach to the future.

You continue to be mentioned by them as a great teacher, having shown how they can make a difference to their own world and then for others. It was equally as thrilling for me to have someone fill in a lot of gaps and yet continue to expand my knowledge in a limitless world of the unknown, reminding me that you don't know what you don't know!

Thanks Zac – if these evenings were to continue, so would we! By the way, if you do them again, we have some more people interested!

Carole V. Auckland New Zealand

I attended Zac's weekly course series, which was an enlightening, fun learning experience. Learning from Zac's vast knowledge and experience that he enthusiastically and generously loved to share, and in a simple way we could all understand was a wonderful. I did not want the course to end. Please, another...... From energy work, health, removing emotional blocks, higher self, meditation, manifesting happiness, subjects too numerous to number. Zac is a walking dictionary on all mind, body, and soul matters. Best wishes on whatever you find the need to follow in the future. Thank you.

Barbara M, Auckland New Zealand.

Table of Contents

Foreward

I call myself the average Joe.

I am 1.8 metres tall pretty average really.

I have an average intelligence quotient.

I am as lazy as the next Joe, but I felt compelled to write a book sharing what I learnt from my time spent with an amazing ageless man called Fabious and some lessons I have learned for myself during my life in this current body.

Disclaimer: This book is a compilation of my own personal life experiences, my own imaginings and my own opinions. Any resemblance to reality commonly experienced by most human beings on this planet is purely coincidental.

My heartfelt hope is that other people will gain a lifetime benefit and value by applying the principles from this book to their lives.

I have divided this book into THREE main parts.

1) Part One – Fabious the man.
2) Part Two – The wisdom of Fabious
3) Part Three – The art of consciously living longer.

The first two parts are about Fabious and outline the spiritual wisdom of Fabious and underpins the spiritual 'head space' a person requires to turn back the aging clock. This wisdom I feel, even though it may not appear to have anything to do with anti-aging is none the less vitally important to grasp. The reason for this is once a person understands on a deep feeling level just how the universe works, what the rules of the game of life are, and how we are indeed the co-creators of our lives, then making the changes in our physical, emotional, mental and spiritual state of being leads to the natural step of anti-aging and becoming more youthful, while creating the type of life we desire.

Part three covers the practical steps to getting younger. It is divided into seven sections. These seven sections are the minimum you will need to adopt and evolve to begin "Youthing" immediately on a cellular level.

"Youthing" means growing younger, as opposed to growing older.

It provides a path to consciously living longer and happier in today's society with all its pressures and stress. It encapsulates Fabious teachings and works on unity at all levels: - physical, mental, emotional and spiritual.

There are two types of aging doctors recognize :

1) Chronological age: This is the actual age of your body.
2) Physiological age: This is the age of the 'wear and tear' for want of a better expression that your body has experienced, thus far. Doctors can measure this age in terms of such things as, blood pressure, heart health, blood circulation, fitness level, muscle strength, skin tone, breathing, hormone production etc. It is quite possible for a person to have a younger or older physiological age than their chronological age.

The purpose of "Youthing " is to reduce your physiological age and thus increase longevity, and to dismantle the ego; thereby freeing up more of the true essence to manifest in your life. *

* Exactly what 'dismantling the ego' and the 'true essence' means will be explained and expanded upon as we progress through the book.

Fabious the Man

Part One

How I met Fabious; the man who drove me out of my mind, quite literally, was inevitable when I look back on it. I am not sure if it is possible to actually go out and seek to find a person like Fabious. It seems to me such a person will find you, if the timing is right. This certainly was the case in my experience. The real story of how I met Fabious starts well over forty years ago.

Since I was a young boy, I have had the ability to see and feel the human aura. I could recall memories of what I have come to call now, past lives. Even at that age the most burning questions I had was about life itself. Why are we here? What's it all about? Is there a God and if so what did God look like? What was God's purpose? What was my purpose in life? For the first twenty years of my life nothing else mattered to me, save these questions and the answers to them.

My friends at school all seemed to know what they wanted to be and do with their lives when they left school. I had no idea. For me, if life was just about being born, growing older, getting a job, getting married, having kids and then dying, then shoot me now, because if that's all there is, then what is the point, I thought.

This motivation lead me on a voracious quest to find out more about "life, the universe and everything," to quote the Hitch Hikers Guide to the Galaxy.

I read many of the books written on most of the religions. The Bible, The Quran, The Bhagavad-Gita, The Upanishad, and The Tarot just to name a few. I looked into all the various types of Yoga including Tantra, Paganism, Wicca, Meditation, Western Mysticism, Occult writings and New Age books of more recent times. My quest also lead me to investigate psychology, group therapy, re-birthing, and to participate in all manner of retreats and workshops. In truth I wanted to make sure that my quest and my obvious "disenchantment" with the explanation of life that society generally teaches us and accepts as reality, was not motivated because I had some deep-seated psychological problem unknown to myself.

I am pleased to say it wasn't. Phew!

Through all this journey and study I started to see the connectivity of these various thoughts, doctrines and religions. I realised that if you remove the zealots within each doctrine and how they behave, and if you don't get hung up on the semantics or the words of each doctrine, they were all basically saying the same thing and delivering the same message, only in different words. After many years on this journey and investigation I realised one very important aspect.

While all my studying gave me an intellectual understanding of how things may be, it was just that: intellectual. I began to realise I would not find the meaning of life while it was based on an intellectual understanding. I began to realise that the 'true' answers all rested *within me* and what I experienced directly on a feeling level – not an intellectual one. And within that direct experience, all of us, can know God, all that there is, universal love, the is-ness; call it what you will. I then entered into a period of my life that others too have experienced. It has been called "the dark night of the soul".

It was during that period that I came to the understanding it was my 'mind' (or ego) itself, the very tool I was employing for my search, which stops me from experiencing directly the universe, (God) directly. I realised that no matter how hard I tried to understand the answers to life, it was my mind (ego) that was doing the trying. The mind, being finite, cannot by definition begin to grasp the infinite directly. This awareness was really quite depressing. It seemed there is this 'secret' that you can almost grasp and fathom but it stays perpetually, tantalizingly, just out of reach.

I realised then, that my 'mind' cannot bring me the ultimate feeling-experience and knowing; of the is-ness that is God. For someone who has never actually done any sky diving, talking all about it, watching a film about it, reading a book about it, while perhaps interesting, will not give them a true 'knowing-ness' of what it is actually like to experience sky diving from an aeroplane. It is just an intellectual exercise; they will never know the experience and reality of it, until they have actually jumped out of a plane themselves.

This was my dark night of the soul.

When I reached this final point, this shattering awareness, I just gave in. I surrendered; I accepted that I would never truly know God, or universal love directly. The dark night is a very lonely, traumatic place to be in. In the depths of this despair I decided, I needed to get away and have a holiday, to think about what I wanted to do with the rest of my life. I needed a time out period. I decided to go to Phuket, in Thailand; a beautiful place, of beaches, sun and surf. It was to be the perfect holiday destination for me to relax and decide what I wanted to do next.

I had decided to give up my quest as being an impossible task, a mere dream, a journey of foolishness made by a fool. Phuket was a restful and fun place to holiday. I spent my days, swimming in its tepid ocean waters, taking elephant treks in the jungle, enjoying the local shows, and learning more of the culture.

At night I enjoyed drinking and dancing to the bands playing in the local restaurants and bars that abound in Phuket. Then it happened. When I least expected it and in truth, wasn't even caring or thinking about anything spiritual whatsoever. One night I was in my now favourite restaurant and bar enjoying the music and out of the corner of my eye I spied a group of people flanking a man as they walked in. When I looked over at this man, our eyes locked and I saw a smile come to his lips. At that point I had a sense my life was about to change. His eyes looked through me but at the same time it felt as if the were taking in the essence of me in that one glance.

I dragged my eyes back to my drink and for the next hour or so I secretly glimpsed over at the man and his followers. One time I looked over and could not see him, he had moved away from the group, it was then I saw a tanned arm and hand reach for the empty chair at my table and the man himself slide athletically into the chair to sit opposite me. I remember his first words to this day.

He looked at me and said, "I have been waiting for you." Something inside of me, and I don't know what it was, made me say, "Sorry I am late, it has been a long trip." Where upon we both broke out into loud, joyous laughter. We spent the rest of that night laughing, dancing and singing songs until the early hours of the morning. As the night drew to its inevitable close, Fabious stood up and announced it was time to leave. At that point I felt an empty feeling in my stomach as if I was a child again who had just had some new toy unexpectedly taken away from him.

I stood and gave my new friends a hug, and of course Fabious himself. When we separated Fabious reached into his jacket pocket and slipped a card into my hand and said, “You must always follow your heart or inner-tuition, come to my house tomorrow.” With that said he smiled at me and turned to his students as they left laughing and full of good humour. I was left alone, so I gathered my jacket from the back of my chair and started the walk back to my hotel. I enjoyed the night air and the smell of the ocean air. As I walked, my mind was trying to understand what my heart had felt during this night and in the meeting with Fabious and his students. My mind kept trying to grab and analyse the night.

Finally, I said “enough” to my own mind as it was just going around and around in circles trying to work out why I felt so, good, so at peace, that night. I decided to let the experience just ‘be’ and enjoy instead the walk and the night. The next morning over breakfast I stared at Fabious’s card I had placed on the table. The address was on the card and from what the hotel concierge had already told me, earlier that morning it was about a 20-minute cab ride from where I was staying. As I moved onto my cup of tea, I reviewed all I had learnt last night from Fabious and the conversations I had with his students regarding life in Fabious’s house.

I remember them saying at any given point there seems to be a fairly stable population of about 50 students. All had been invited to Fabious house; it seemed that no one could stay unless invited. As I remembered those words I felt proud that I had been invited and I also chuckled to myself at my own inflated ego for having such thoughts. Some students had been there a long time I gathered, and some not so long. Students often left on some trip or other, perhaps to visit back home and then they returned. The students themselves seem to be a mixed bag of races. Some were locals and many, most in fact, were foreign students from all countries and walks of life. I remember later we would sometimes call ourselves a mini United Nations! As I sat there over my tea I was in two minds. My heart felt it was the place for me to go but my head had doubts. Even the possibility that this was some clever cult trying to drag innocent travellers into its mix had occurred to me.

I thought also, about all that I had been searching for up to this point in my life and the reason I had come to be in Thailand in the first place. As I thought along those lines a certain feeling of inevitability and rightness came over me, that I should indeed go to visit and stay, at least for a short time in Fabious's presence.

How long that time would end up being: I knew not, at that point. I certainly didn't have any pressing reason to go back home. The moment had come when I realised that no matter what my head said and what doubts it still had, it would be my heart that day, that would win its way and I thank the universe to this day, for making that decision. I didn't know it then, just how many amazing changes were to enter my being, as I got up from the table to go and pack my belongings and then check out of my hotel room.

This then, was how I met Fabious. And the day I became his student. It was the beginning of the next, and most profound chapter of my life, where all of the puzzles, the questions, my obsessive searching, came to fruition. It was the start of a period of time after which I was never the same again. Miracles (Some described in detail later in book) entered my life on this day. Looking back with the benefit of 20/20 hindsight vision I realised that all I had done previously in my life, all the struggle and searching were merely the preparation period to make this time with Fabious possible. Nothing was wasted; each and every experience had had its purpose.

So who is this Fabious? ……………..

Fabious's age was very hard to determine and when asked, he invariably skirted the subject. Sometimes he seemed very young with his easy laughter and almost childlike fascination with life and at other times, I felt that he was quite ancient, especially when he spoke with such wisdom.

Fabious was like no other man I had ever met before.

At times I wondered if he was SO holy (or whole) that we mortal students didn't really understand just how holy he was. Or was he, indeed, just a mortal man touched with a madness that confounded our minds and challenged our beliefs? Did we choose to see what we wanted to see in him and therefore by extension, come to see the potential that lay within ourselves?

In the end, did it really matter who or what he was? Fabious taught me that: "On one level nothing really matters and on another, everything matters" …just one of his many cryptic sayings! Fabious was a man of average height, in his 40's, chronologically; with black hair, olive skin, and no other physically striking or distinguishing features. He was extremely fit and healthy - attested to by the strange exercises he had all his students perform every morning before breakfast. There was not a single day in the next five years that Fabious was in my life, that he didn't have the group of us, his 'students', stretching, contorting and moving our bodies. The body, he would say, is: *"The anchor of the soul that binds it to this earthly plane."* Three days a week after our morning exercises, he would gather us all together and run with us into the hills surrounding the village to his favourite resting place with superb views back down the wooded valley to the village below.

During these times he would extol,

"The body is a vessel and we are merely its tenants. Like all good tenants we must keep it as clean and as perfect as it was the day we took possession, lest the landlord toss us out before our lease is truly finished!"

At other times, Fabious would have us sit quietly, waiting and willing our minds into a peacefulness where the whole world could be seen and understood from the top of this peaceful knoll - his 'time-out' place. Physically, as I have said, he was nothing extraordinary. However he did have three things about him that set him apart, and gave him, at times, a mystical sense of *other worldliness*. These were his fathomless eyes, his enigmatic smile and his hypnotic voice.

His voice was rich and smooth, flowing like water over our student ears. It drew us to him, upwards and forwards, away from our worldly cares, worries and fears. It really didn't matter what subject Fabious spoke about, we all eagerly drank in his words, like thirsty men in a desert. Sometimes I had the impression that even the birds stopped singing, the better to hear him talk. It was years later when I realised it was not only what he was saying that had its profound effect but it was also the vibrations of the actual 'sounds' of the words that had their own effect. Fabious taught us that words have an innate power in themselves - a vibration or resonance, if you like, and we must all learn to husband and guard whatever utterances we make, lest the effect be one of disharmony, discord and chaos rather than harmony, balance and order.

Fabious taught us over and over again the simple truth: "Wise is the man who guards his tongue and so can release the power of his spoken word." It is said that the eyes are the windows of the soul. And if Fabious' eyes were indeed that, then his soul was liquid nirvana. To look into his eyes was to lose your very soul in those deep pools. It was as if you were standing naked in front of him and your every secret flaw, mean spirited thought or action, was laid bare before him. His eyes were filled with total acceptance and compassion. He never judged or frowned.

Rather, his eyes bathed you in love and it felt as if all the burdens and hang-ups you carried within were suddenly washed away, and you emerged virgin once more, innocent and ready to start life again with a clean slate. When Fabious spoke, his rich voice combined with his powerful expression and his deep fathomless eyes, made it seem he was speaking to you alone, though the room was filled with students. The tales he told of history came alive and the senses it seemed were transported back in time and space to whatever and wherever Fabious was talking about. He spoke with such passion and conviction you would have sworn he had been an actual witness to each event. And his smile; Fabious had a magical smile that could light up a room, and he used it often. He found humour and laughter in most things in life.

He said we took ourselves far too seriously.

"This moment is all we have. What happened yesterday and what may happen tomorrow are nothing more than memories and possibilities. The' now' we experience is all we have, so it is best to choose to laugh, to have joy and be happy every "now moment." To Fabious, life was like a play and we were nothing more than actors. "So enjoy the acting," he would say. "Be the very best actor you can be, by all means, but never lose sight of the fact that you are, indeed, only acting."

He taught us that if we were planning some momentous event or dealing with something serious, a crisis perhaps, that had struck our lives, then we should act like an actor, taking it very seriously making the very best decisions possible, but never forgetting that we are just actors role-playing at taking life seriously. It took me a long time to understand what he meant. I began to practise observing myself being serious, angry or sad and being happy, ecstatic and joyful as well. Fabious said that he would always choose the happy emotions over the sad ones any day.

Fabious was very earthy in his likes and desires. Not for him, the path of purity and denial of the flesh. Once a week he would take us into the village to relax, to laugh, sing, dance and play with the local villagers who loved him dearly. On those days he would eat, drink and be merry in ways that would curl the tonsured heads of the holy men from a neighbouring village monastery.

When asked why, he would laugh loudly and say, "Life is about balance and to deny aspects of oneself is to bring a canker into your being."

To enjoy the friendship and fellowship of your friends and neighbours is a chance to exchange energy of the highest possible kind. All parties in every relationship must benefit. In these times, he was still Fabious, kind, light-hearted, humorous, filled with delight and I am sure he was secretly standing back observing that part of himself having so much fun. He would say: "Be wary of the person who after some wine changes his personality dramatically, for they are not being true to their inner nature."

So this was Fabious our teacher. He would never allow us to call him master for he said, "No one is anyone's master. The only master a person can have, is themselves."

A day in the life ……

Our life with Fabious was fairly ordered. Each day started in the common room where he put us through our morning contortions, and body movements. Three days a week he would lead us on a run into the hills to listen to his words, or to meditate in peace and solitude. After breakfast, the first of six meals each day, we would each begin our work for the day. Most of us would head for the communal gardens to begin work. Some would do maintenance or building work, some would go to the kitchens and those who had been with Fabious a while would work with him, healing those who came to his house in need.

Fabious would allow no one to remain idle during the day. He taught: "*A man without work is like a ship without direction. It is our work that keeps us in step with nature and a man feels fulfilment when working, creating, and contributing. Just as the planet turns and one season follows another, in tune with the wheel of life, so the 'right' work keeps a man centred, in tune and happy.*" It does not matter what the work you do is, as long as fulfilment comes from it and everyone involved, benefits.

Fabious said: "*Each person must find the 'right' work for themselves. Each soul incarnated on this planet has some unique gift, ability, talent that he should strive to identity and once identified, strive to perfect and once perfected, make this his life's work.*"

Work such as this ceases to become work. It becomes a passion, a pleasure and this is when humans feel most fulfilment. I remember one student asking, "How does one know when one is performing his 'right' work?"

Fabious replied: "Each soul has its unique lessons in life to learn. You know instinctively when you are learning these lessons and the way you know you are doing the "right" work is very, very simple...."

.... he paused and smiled mischievously. He knew we were all leaning forward listening intently with expectation, and we were also aware he was teasing us.

Fabious smiled again and said,

"You can tell if you are performing your right work and if you are learning your lessons by simply asking yourself this question: Are you having many more happy days than unhappy days? If the answer is 'yes' congratulations! If the answer is 'no' then change what you do for work. My students it is as simple as that. "*You are all fine people whom I love dearly but your minds expect everything to be complicated and think there is some 'secret' answer to enlightenment that has to be wrestled with and can only be reached after much hardship and pain, but it is not so. The simple fact is in the answer to that question. Are you having more happy days than unhappy days? If Yes – congratulations you are getting on with doing what you are meant to be doing. If No then change."*

With that Fabious stood up and disappeared to do a healing on the local village mayor's son, who had arrived at the community house. At times like this, we students would look at each other and burst out laughing at the simple truth that had touched our souls in that moment. The rest of the day usually continued for me, working in the gardens with my fellow students. Evening would come as evening does and after the dinner meal, the fifth one for the day, we would once more congregate in the communal room.

We would laugh and joke together, some would bring instruments to play and sing too, some students would write letters or write in their journals. We generally and genuinely enjoyed the fellowship of each other's company. We always looked forward to the magic 8 o'clock hour. This was when Fabious would join us. He would spend a short period of time laughing and joking with us. He would then compose himself as we composed ourselves, and the evening teaching would commence for an hour or so before we had our late supper and retired for the night.

The format for these teachings varied from day to day. Sometimes a student would ask some questions and Fabious would speak on them for the evening. Other times Fabious would lead us in a group meditation. Often he would take some chalk and on a large slate proceed to write either a saying or a verse of some kind. He would then have us relax our minds in meditation for five or so minutes, and ask us each in our mind's eye to read the saying or verse and take some time to contemplate our own meaning and understanding of the it. After twenty minutes had passed in such manner, Fabious would begin to discuss it.

I suspect that Fabious never knew exactly what each night's lesson would end up being but as he used to tell us: "It is the journey that holds the key and it is the fun experienced along the way that is the lesson." So I think it suited his free flowing teaching method. It was during these lessons and shared times that I felt most uplifted. All I did each day was done to sustain these evening talks. I am sure the other students felt this way as well. One was never quite the same after experiencing one of Fabious's talks. Looking back I realise each talk was opening our minds, expanding them, further and further, but in an integrated way. When the lesson had finished, Fabious would have us meditate again for twenty minutes.

The long busy day would finish with supper, after which we would retire for a good nights rest. That was life when living with Fabious. In "part two" of the following section are some of Fabious's talks and teachings from those evenings. While they can never be as good as hearing them directly from Fabious himself, I hope that they convey to you some of his wisdom.

The Wisdom Of Fabious

Part Two

I remember a student asked once, **"What is the difference between men and women?"** Fabious smiled as he often did, and said, "*I am assuming you are not referring to the obvious physical differences. The short answer is that in a man and woman's essential self there is no difference. The spark of life, the soul, the essence of the two sexes is exactly the same. Our essential selves come from the one source of God stuff. This God stuff is the original source of all there is. It is the primordial soup from which everything derives including life itself. Before we incarnate however, on a soul level we analyse and choose the circumstances of our birth. We do this in order to be born into an environment that will best enable us to learn the lessons we have chosen for ourselves this time round or sometimes to pay off our karmic debts in the best way possible. Or a combination of both.*

We choose such factors as who our parents will be, what country we will be born in, our horoscope (the word itself means 'right time'), for our time of birth and even the name we will be given by our parents. Significantly we choose what sex we will be, as we leave the higher vibration level of the soul and fully move into the foetus, at three months. Remember, dear students, in the spiritual realm there is only one reality and that is unity. There is one essence. It is on the earth plane that the illusion of duality occurs. For the purposes of this discussion I refer specifically to the illusion of the duality of masculinity and femininity."

We must now look at the 'qualities' embraced by each of these aspects.

In their purest form they are as follows. The feminine aspect encompasses: - openness, receptivity, listening, nurturing, intuition, friendship, emotion, feeling, art, comprehension, creativity, holism, stillness, silence, tranquillity, calm, introversion, fluidity and flexibility.

The male aspect encompasses: - protectiveness, eagerness, outward focus,, strength, action, competitiveness, objectivity, logic, linearity, analytical ability, rationality, expansiveness, clear seeing, precision, extroversion, structure and form. All these are aspects of femininity and masculinity and generally the male has more of the male aspects and a woman the female aspects. We must learn to balance both these energies within us. When the sexes interrelate, one with the other, each has their particular aspects to teach the other and so help their partner develop a balance of these forces within their own being.

If you asked five friends, who know you well, to describe how they find you to be, the list they present to you, with their descriptive words, will reveal to you how well balanced the yin and yang, male and female aspects are within you.

Would your list have roughly an equal amount of male and female aspects and attributes? Or is there a major leaning one way or the other in your friends' perception of you? The balance or lack of balance can be a measuring stick of your progress along the path and an indicator on what you need to work on to achieve more balance in your life.

Fabious paused for a few moments and then said, *"I will now reveal the sexual differences between the female and male aspects and how these differences can be used to further your spiritual growth.*" He laughed and added, "*I am not talking about the physical sexual body differences but rather the spiritual sexual body differences. Within the human body dear students as I have taught and shown you, there are seven, major Chakra. They are the same in both male and female. The first is the lower or sexual Chakra situated between the anus and sexual organs, the next is the social and emotional Chakra found just below the navel, and then the intellectual Chakra near the solar plexus region. Above this is the love Chakra, near the heart region, then the expressive Chakra near the throat, and above this the intuition or physic Chakra, also called the third eye, in the middle of the forehead. Finally, the spiritual Chakra at the crown of the head.* (See later in book for more details)

To complicate things further, at the bottom resting in the lower Chakra is what has been called the Kundalini. Think of it as a ball of energy that resides there waiting to be awakened. That ball of energy feeds the lower Chakra and so if you like dissipates sideways in a small-localised ball of energy. However it is possible for that energy to become focussed and move up the spinal column and as it does so it activates and energises all the Chakra as it moves through them towards the crown Chakra. After a time of foreplay when the male inserts his penis into a woman's vagina, a process begins and as the woman begins building towards her orgasm, the male energy stimulates this Kundalini energy to start moving up each successive Chakra of the woman cumulating with her orgasm in her crown Chakra.

At that moment a clairvoyant looking would see a whirlpool type funnel in the astral opening up from the woman's crown Chakra. When a woman has an orgasm there is a moment in time when a woman has no concept of her ego-self, she becomes 'self-less' as it were, lost totally in the experience of that 'now' moment. By doing so she has opened the funnel to the 'essence' force and that force starts to be channelled down the whirlpool through her Chakra from top to bottom, right back down to her lower Chakra. Now usually what has happened by that time is the male has also climaxed and he has withdrawn his penis from the woman. He is overcome with a sense of tiredness and often, much to the complaint of woman, falls asleep."

Fabious's chuckle filled the room, followed by knowing smiles from some of the female students in the room. Fabious continued. "*What should happen is that after a male has had his orgasm, inside his partner's vagina he should remain inside her to allow his penis to become flaccid naturally, so it comes out after a time of its own accord.*

During this period what will happen is the 'essence' energy coming back down via the woman's crown Chakra will reach her lower Chakra and jump across to his lower Chakra and move up his spinal cord and Chakra *cumulating in his crown Chakra being stimulated and fed by this "essence" energy. The male has lifted the woman up to that spiritual level to make contact and she has brought that essence down into this earth plane to feed the male. Three outcomes occur. One, both male and female have balanced out the male and female forces within themselves. Two, intimacy between the couple is in the calming down period. Three, the male is re-energised and will find he won't need to fall asleep."* With those last words, Fabious smiled, and said that the night's lesson was finished.

On another occasion a student asked, **"What is the "ego" you talk of"?**

Fabious looked around the room at the gathered students and asked, "*How many of us are collected here in this room?*" A student looked around and you could see him counting heads, after a moment he said "forty seven."

Fabious smiled and said, "*There is exactly one. The 'ego-us' is what creates the illusion we think of as this world. Everything you think you are: You are not. It is our ego that creates the illusion of duality. It delights in creating an 'us' and 'them' mentality. This is theirs and that is mine, this is good and that is bad. This is right and that is wrong. It is the ego that creates the feeling of I, me and mine. Everything you currently think of as being you is the ego and the "ego-you" constantly evaluates all your sensory inputs, and all that happens to you, from that perspective.*

The "ego-you" has been growing since the day you were born and even before that time. All your past experiences good or bad have shaped the "ego-you". The "ego-you" colours your experiences of the world on all levels, be they physical, mental, emotional or spiritual. The "ego-you" is looking at the world through tinted glasses, which only allows through the lenses that which confirms your "ego-you" held belief systems.

You think you are, for example: -

A man, a woman, a husband, a wife, a parent, a businessperson, a pastry cook, a fireman, a builder or whatever.

Your "ego-you" measures success in terms of the car you drive, the house you live in, the clothes you wear, the jewellery you display, and the intellect you have or are admired for, your sporting prowess, the body you have chiselled and yes, even the mind you use. All is ego. All are illusions and it is a thin curtain that separates you from your true self; - your essence. While the "ego-you" exists, then separateness, from the essence, exists. The fact is that the larger your ego is, the more you are separated from your essence. The greater you are separated from your essence, the more unhappiness the "ego-you" experiences. People have achieved what the ego world considers to be great success, wealth, fame, property, cars, jewellery, many glamorous sexual partners - all the ego should need to be fulfilled and yet they have not been happy. In fact in some ways the realisation of these material possessions can make them unhappier for once achieved, they then wonder why they are not indeed truly happy."

Fabious smiled and said, "*There is nothing wrong with these baubles, don't get me wrong, but believing that these will bring you happiness is an illusion. See the baubles as baubles and don't become attached to them with the 'ego-you"'*

I will give you an analogy. Imagine a modern house and imagine the power lines leading into the house. Imagine now the electricity pouring down the power lines and into the house. Imagine this electricity as being the essence, the real you. The electricity is a connected flow or energy. It enters the house and from there it starts to inhabit, energise, animate and bring to life various objects. A heater, a stove, a train set, a toaster, a kettle, a computer etc. Now imagine after a period of time the train set starts to take on a pseudo life of its own and it starts to think of itself as a train set and it starts to identify and create a mindset, that it is a train set.

It completely forgets it is the electricity, it even forgets that if it weren't for the electricity still entering into itself, it would cease to be. It takes on a whole false viewpoint on life and its environment completely sure that its perspective in life is the only one and the best. It says to itself, "Look at me, aren't I great? I have all these moving parts and I can send things all around this room." It looks over at the heater and says, "poor creature, it has to stay in one place and all it does is heat a room." The heater, meantime, has also taken on its own pseudo life and looks at the train and says "poor creature, destined to go round in cycles for the rest of its life."

Now imagine one day after many days, months, years (lifetimes for us) the train starts to think, "There must be more to life than just this!" Imagine over time it goes deeper into itself and starts to discover that there is an internal source or power or energy greater than itself and over time starts to realise that, that "essence" is its real self. Eventually it starts to realise that even what it is thinking with, is also not its real self. Eventually it starts to accept the idea that in order to know its real self then all that it used to think it was, was nothing but an illusion As it journeys down this path, flashes of insight start to manifest themselves. The way it looks at life changes slowly but surely.

Suddenly it realises that the heater it had looked down upon in the past is also made of the same essence stuff and in that way it is no different than itself. The train's ego and sense of 'self-centeredness' is eroded and grows smaller and smaller and as it does so the expression of essence and the feeling of essence increases more and more. Then one day, the ego of the train disintegrates and it is suddenly thrust away from the train-set itself and is just the essence in pure expression."

Fabious paused, and looked around the room meeting the eyes of each student present in turn. He said, "*There is no need for me to say that the electricity is the essence, the real you, your god self. The physical train and the heater is the physical earth plane manifestation and the mind of the train is the ego-us."*

Fabious stood and stretched, then walked to the white board and wrote:

"*Here is a simple test to see how well you are progressing on your journey, dear students.*" Then he wrote: "*Remember self-honesty is an integral part of a spiritual journey.*" He turned to us, looking over his shoulder and smiled in his Fabious way and said, "*When you drop your current body you will go to a place where you will review all you have done in this lifetime, the good, the bad, the indifferent and on that day you will be your own judge and jury. So you may as well practice now,"* he laughed loudly.

Turning back to the white board he wrote. "*Score yourself from zero to ten on the following statements. Zero means you never feel a certain way described in each of them, and ten means you always feel that way described in the statements. Or choose a number in between that best represents how often you feel that way in your life.*"

1) I feel envious or jealous of what other people have or what other people can do.
2) I get angry often.
3) I defend my point of view strongly when others disagree with me.
4) I need to be right all the time.
5) I have to control people I am in close relationships with.
6) I don't trust people of a different religion, social standing, ethnic background.
7) I worry all the time that something bad will happen, and I assume the worst will happen in any given situation.
8) I am anxious about life and what it will bring to me next.
9) I don't like trying new things, learning new ways to do things, like learning to dance for example, due to a fear of making a fool out of myself in public.
10) I get upset when people around me do not follow the social protocols. .
11) I fear failing in life so sometimes I don't attempt to achieve new goals or try new things.
12) If someone says something bad about me I take it to heart and feel devastated.
13) I have a burning desire to be liked by everyone I meet.

14) If I lost my car, my house, my work, my money, I would be totally devastated and life would not be worth living.
15) I tend to put people into categories. They are either higher up the success ladder than I am or lower or about the same.
16) I only see one point of view – mine.
17) I meet a lot of people in a given week that rub me up the wrong way.
18) It is important to me that people see me as kind, generous, loving and that they hold me in high regard.
19) I get upset easily when things don't work out the way I had planned and can act like a spoilt brat at these times.
20) I seek revenge against those that I perceive to have been mean to me or have maligned me in some way.

Fabious turned from the board and said, "*Now add your scores up and divide by twenty. That is your score: - obviously the lower the score the more you have chipped away at your ego.*" Fabious then smiled and said, "*I would wager that the people with the lower scores have more enjoyment and happiness in their lives as well – strange that!*" "*As a matter of interest,*" Fabious said, "*Another useful exercise, is to imagine yourself as you were say, ten years ago and go through these questions again answering them as you think you would have answered them then..*" It is a way of seeing for yourself how much progress you have made or not made along the path in the last ten years.

With that Fabious declared the night's lesson over and walked out of the common room leaving us to wonder about our scores and, with some irony, wonder what the other students' scores were. This made me laugh hard and long at myself, for I suddenly realised how my own ego was trapping me and playing tricks on me yet again.

One evening a student asked, **"If God, the essence, always was, always will be, and encompasses everything there is; if it already knows everything, that can happen, will happen and if our 'true' nature is also made up of, and comes from, this God stuff, why did the essence separate itself and incarnate into the illusion of appearing as limited individual beings like ourselves?"**

I looked around at the faces of some of the other students gathered and could tell that they too, had been contemplating this very question. My attention returned to Fabious who was looking into the faces of us all.. As I looked at him I became overwhelmed with a deep sense of compassion pouring from his eyes; so kind and loving. "*That, dear students, is a very good question,*" said Fabious, as he stood up from his chair and moved to stand in front of the student who had asked the question.

"*To answer that question I will give you all a very loose analogy that may shed some light on this matter,*" he said. Fabious held up his hands in front of the student's face and said, "*Imagine for the moment that your head represents all that there is and all that ever will be. It is of infinite size and exists everywhere at once in time and space and all levels of vibrations.*"

After saying that, Fabious drew an imaginary square with his hands, in a box-like shape around the student's head. "*So now your head represents the essence, the God stuff. You have no body, no legs, no arms, just your head and that represents God.*"

Looking directly at the student and speaking to him alone, Fabious said, "*Now, dear student, imagine for some reason, just for the pleasure of it, you, remember you now (in this analogy, you are the essence, you are God), you decide that it would be 'fun' to experience yourself in many varied ways.*

Say, for instance, you want to experience what colour your eyes were or what the skin below your nose looked like, or what shape your ears were. So you decide to manifest a 'tool' or a vehicle to fully experience these attributes about yourself." Looking directly into the students eyes Fabious asked, "*What tool could you invent that would answer these questions?"* The student looked puzzled and thought for a moment and said, "*I would create a mirror."* Fabious smiled and said, "*Yes, you well might."*

Fabious now drew a square box in front of the students face. *"Here is your mirror and now you can begin to experience the colour of your eyes, the tone of your skin below your nose, the shape of your ear*s," he said. *"Is the image looking out from the mirror you*?" Fabious asked the student. "No" the student answered, "*It is but a reflection of me*." Fabious smiled and asked, "*Did you not, out of your essence, create the mirror?" "Yes*" said the student. *"Did you not also create the laws of reflection so you can see the image in the mirror?"* Fabious further asked. Again the student said, *"Yes."*

"So the reflection though not a full representation of the entire essence of you, still comes entirely from you and represents, therefore, aspects of you, albeit a somewhat limited aspect, does it not?" Fabious asked. "*Yes, I guess so*," said the student. "*Now imagine, dear student, that, as God, you decide to put a small part of yourself into that image in the mirror to animate it, just like a child may put a battery into a computer robot toy so it can walk and talk."* As Fabious walked back to his seat he motioned the student that he may sit down now as well. Fabious resumed talking.

"Now imagine that time passes and over time the reflection forgets that it is indeed not real at all and it loses all contact with this inner understanding. It forgets that its very power source is God. It forgets it exists on the other side of a mirror. It forgets it is a pale reflection of what is real. It starts to create its own reality on the other side of the mirror, and develop its own ego-based persona and interpretation of its own perception of reality. If you were wondering, students, then, yes, the essence did know this very thing would happen," Fabious chuckled.

"Now God can look on with fun and interest to see how the game progresses. How will his creation work its way out of the mirror? How creative will the robot toy become? What adventures will it have along the path? When will it free itself from the maze? What will be the high points and low points of its illusionary existence? Who will realise that they are more than a limited being behind a mirror first and what will they do with this knowledge when they start to interrelate with others behind the mirror? Dear students, we (the ego lower we) are ALL nothing more than a reflection in the mirror, that is God. "Our mission is to escape the mirror and merge back with our true essence, which is God."

Fabious paused, took a drink of his water and looked around the room at his students. "*You can see now, why the measuring stick of our progress in escaping from this mirror, can be gauged by how many good and happy days we have in life as opposed to bad and unhappy days. If God is conducting this great experiment for the fun of it, then it follows that we, as a reflection of God, by following the paths that give us the most inner fulfilment and fun in our lives, will be naturally working our way out of the mirror. If God set this whole scenario up in the first place just for the fun of it, then doing what brings us the most fun and fulfilment, has to be the road map, the guide line, the path that leads us out of this game of life we play."*

Fabious then called this evening to a close and proceeded to lead us into a 20-minute meditation on the analogy he had shared with us this night. When we had finished he stood up and walked towards the door half way there, he turned around and casually said, " *I wonder if that's why humans have always thought it was bad luck to break mirrors,"* whereupon he burst out laughing. I could hear his chuckles as he strode away from the meeting room leaving us totally bemused by his parting comment.

After being away for a while I remember one student asked Fabious on his return: **"When I went home and visited my parents I went for a walk. On that walk I came across a man teaching his students in a field. He was telling them of a set of disciplines and a way of life very different to what you are teaching us Fabious. I spoke to his students afterwards and they said that theirs was the only way of knowing the essence – God. My question is: Is there only one way to know the essence or are there many ways, and if so how can that be?"**

Fabious smiled and learned back comfortably in his chair.

After a moment thought, he said, "*Firstly dear students, it is important that you understand the old saying: - There are many ways up the mountain but the view from the top is the same. How you get to the top is not as important as actually getting there and enjoying the view. "Our egos cause us all to have different personalities, different attitudes, different constitutions, different ways and attitudes of mind. Ultimately as we journey up the mountain our lower-self egos diminish and finally disappear altogether as we become pure channels of the essence on this plane. The reason there are many ways up the mountain is that different paths suit different personalities.*

For one person leading an austere life, of self-denial and hardship is the best way for them to get rid of the burden of their ego. For another person, that path would not work, nor is it needed and they would need an entirely different path up the mountain; perhaps even one that is the complete opposite. However, both paths lead, eventually, up the mountain. It is like taking a journey, one person flies in an old-fashioned bi-plane, while another flies in a twin engine, air conditioned jet. As long as both planes reach the destination then how they travelled is irrelevant.

Every path has its place and ultimately people must choose their own path. Sometimes they may follow one path for a while and later change to a different one as they work on reducing their ego and their needs change. To say that only one particular path is the right and only path, is spoken from a very limited state of consciousness and one of spiritual bankruptcy," Fabious said shaking his head in an amused manner, with a smile on his face.

"Unfortunately more wars, more strife and crimes against humanity have been caused in the name of defending one particular path of spirituality over another, than for any other single reason in mankind's history. That is somewhat ironic to say the least," Fabious sadly said.

"*As you climb up the mountain and your ego lessens and you begin to have more of the essence flowing through you and less of the ego, you start to reach a point of clarity – perhaps it is that the view gets wider and you can perceive the connectivity of all things. When you look back down the mountain you can clearly see all the winding paths, each with pilgrims like yourself, trudging ever upwards. You perceive that these other pilgrims are your brothers and sisters, and all are striving to reach the same peak. You will feel an overwhelming love and respect for each one, no matter what height they have achieved so far, and your very best hopes for them will flow down towards them."*

Fabious became quiet for a moment then he led us into a meditation on this concept. For some reason that night as I lay in bed my thoughts were very sober and I thought about how selfish I still was. The talk had hit home with me, on a deep level that night. I felt a sense of how far I still have to go to get up that mountain. Looking within myself I realised how much 'spiritual pride' ego I had. I noticed how my 'clever, cunning ego' had carved out a hiding place for itself under the very guise of being spiritual.

After a particularly busy day of people coming to the house for healing I remember a student asked: **"How does your healing actually work?"** Fabious smiled and said, "*As I have taught you, we don't inhabit only one body but in fact we inhabit seven bodies at once. Each body co-exists with, and is interpenetrating the other bodies, each one vibrating at a higher level than the one that precedes it.* (*See later in book for more details*)

The body immediately above the physical body in vibration is called the etheric body and the one above that in vibration is the aura or astral body. I principally work on the etheric body and to a degree the astral body but more the etheric body. You can think of the etheric body as being superimposed over, around and inside the physical body and extending out from the human body by a few inches or so. Its shape is similar to the human form. The etheric body is like a blue print for the human body. It is the perfect template, model or picture of the human body that is supremely healthy and in perfect balance in all ways and aspects.

It is important to remember that the human body wants to be healthy, and manifest on the physical plane the perfect shape that the etheric body represents. This is one of the main reasons for 'Phantom pains' experienced by people who have lost a leg.. They keep registering pain as if the leg still remained. This is because the physical body is still trying to conform to the etheric pattern of the limb.

It is one of the few times when I have to work on changing the etheric pattern to conform to the new physical body shape. Most times the work is the other way round, getting the body to realign with the perfect etheric body. The reason humans experience poor health is that the body has moved away from this perfect template.

Things that cause the body to move away from the perfect template are:-

1) *Physical – actual damage to body, strains in the body, broken bones, unhealthy eating and drinking habits, drugs, air pollution, insecticides eaten with food etc.*
2) *Mental – work stress, relationship stress, stress in general, not having fulfilling work etc.*
3) *Emotional – excessive worry, conflict in drives and goals, not being true to ourselves, suppression of feelings, not expressing ourselves etc.*
4) *Spiritual – not sensing or getting on with your chosen life's lessons, not living within the essence, being completely out of touch with your own true nature.*

So I take each person as an individual and help them to resolve whichever area of conflict they are experiencing from these four categories. Once this is done I then allow the essence to flow through me into the patient's etheric body to strengthen it, then via the etheric body, the essence flows into the physical body. The essence then restores the physical body to the shape and robustness of the etheric body."

Fabious smiled and asked the student, *"Does that answer your question*?" "Yes, thank you" the student replied. At that the night's lesson was brought to a close.

On another occasion a student asked, **"What is Karma and how does it actually work?"** *"Karma has been described as a huge wheel that inextricably grinds ever onwards,"* Fabious responded. "*Karma is cosmic balance and Karma is on its way to producing neutrality in manifestation."*

The essence, – God if you like - is above and beyond. It is not subject to Karma. God is everything manifested and is all things not yet manifested. God is potential unlimited. All things stem from and return to the essence.

So you see Karma has nothing to do with God being kind to some people and harsh to others. Karma came into play when human egos came into play. They arrived simultaneously. Ego creates Karma and Karma shapes ego. The ultimate aim is to dismantle the ego completely and thus cease Karma and create neutrality. Fabious continued, *"In some ways, dear students, you can look upon us as having two parts in one body. On the one hand we have our 'lower self' which is very strongly ego based and selfish and on the other hand we have our 'higher self' which is less ego orientated and more essence driven and is accordingly less selfish and able to see the whole spiritual picture.*

We have all had the experience of choosing a course of action and even as we choose that course of action we know we are doing it for the wrong reasons. It is as if a higher part of us knows instinctively what is right and just. This is our higher self-talking to us. Too often we ignore it at our peril. But remember, even the higher self is still an ego and ultimately it, too, must make the ultimate sacrifice and disappear as we journey up the mountain. The larger our ego and the more we interrelate in life from our lower ego selves perspectives and motivations, then generally the more Karma we build up along the way.

When we leave this current body, we go to a place where our higher selves evaluate our experiences, decisions, actions and words; what we said and what we did in the Earth life we have just left behind. In this place our higher selves, through what is called the Akashic records, know everything our lower self did, thought or experienced, in that last life, including, importantly as far as Karma goes, the motivations behind all our decisions." Fabious paused and took a drink of water and stretched his legs before continuing. *"It is no one but ourselves, our higher selves that is the judge and jury. Our higher self is at the hub of the Karmic wheel. It is the place where we decide to go back and relearn lessons if needed or to go back and make amends in some fashion for our actions from the pervious life, sometimes we volunteer to experience certain things to help those around us who have lessons to learn about themselves. This is quite a selfless act but a learning opportunity for us as well, none the less. So you see, dear students, the wheel of Karma does go round but it is driven and created by us, ourselves, our lower selves, and it is our higher selves that decide the atonement and Karma needed or due. One thing I should mention about Karma is that it doesn't have to manifest itself exactly as you have dished it out. For example, I may be mean or horrible to one person today, and, yes, someone may well be mean and horrible to me next week. However, equally, I may end up with a boil or skin rash the following day. Karma, in fact, often comes back in disguised forms but come back it* will *in some fashion.*

The second thing," continued Fabious, *"to be aware of, my friends, is that as you travel higher up the mountain, Karma comes back to the advancing soul much quicker than it does to someone lower on the mountain. So, as you progress, you must be aware of this fact and increasingly you must act out of only the purest of motivations."* Fabious closed his eyes for a moment, then leaned forward and said, *"We should also ask, how do we transcend the law of karma? How do we get out from under its yolk? How can we have our past Karma instantly released, forgiven and wiped clean? How can we stop creating Karma?"*

Fabious looked into the eyes of each student Remember the simple rule, all thoughts, words and actions will have a Karmic effect, good or bad. Before each decision or action you take, stop for a moment and ask yourself 'will this benefit all the people involved?' If the answer is yes, you are fairly safe; if the answer is no, then think how you can modify the decision or action. Until you reach the state of reality where the ego-you, no longer exists, and only pure essence pours through you, you will incur Karma. By following that simple rule, you will incur the least amount of Karma possible. Oh and one last point, dear students. Rising above all Karma is your ultimate release from Karma and this means bad Karma obviously but it also includes good Karma. For good Karma is still a debt. The name of the game is to achieve the neutrality of manifestation, for as I mentioned ultimately God, the essence, the real you is above Karma.

This does not mean that you should avoid performing 'good' actions, because chances are you need the brownie points," laughed Fabious, which made us all laugh as well. "It is just that when you perform a good deed, think of it as a gift to the universe and expect nothing in return. Practice the art of giving as a pure gift. Whatever your actions, deeds, thoughts or words are, make them pure." Fabious then led us into a twenty-minute meditation on tonight's lesson before declaring the lesson closed.

It was on a powerful and somewhat frightening thunderstorm night that a student rather aptly asked, **"Is there really good and evil and such a thing as the Devil in this world?"** Fabious leaned back in his chair, looked up and said, "No". He then remained silent. After a period we students started to look around at each other obviously uncomfortable in the silence. Fabious burst out laughing and said, "Oh, you wanted the long, drawn out answer, did you?" Fabious loved to tease us.

"Firstly, dear students, we must identify what is real, what is absolute, and what is illusion. The only absolute is as follows…." Fabious leaned forward to emphasis what he was about to say. *"There is only one essence, one God if you like. This one essence is aware of itself. This essence encompasses all that there is. It exists everywhere at once, in both time and in space and in all dimensions. It has nothing it particularly has to do and it has nowhere it particularly has to go, for it is already everywhere at once and it has all potential within itself already.*

That is the only absolute. Everything else is illusion.

This illusion is created by our ego.

It is our ego that attributes meaning and importance to the things and events in our lives." Fabious looked deep into my eyes and it was as if the importance of this single concept was pouring from him into my very being and depths. Fabious continued, " Because the essence is everything, and everything that we perceive has come out of this essence, then it is ludicrous, absurd, and illogical to talk of 'another' separate being (which humans have labelled 'The Devil') that could somehow manifest itself out of the same essence. The Devil is really the human ego's refusal to take responsibility for the selfish acts it performs. It is much more palatable to blame 'The Devil' for all the suffering and evil in the world.

The judgement of good and evil is made by human egos. If something happens that suits our ego, then that is labelled good, if it doesn't suit, then it is labelled bad. In the extreme it is called evil." Fabious paused and took a sip of water. He continued, "Countries have applied this principle throughout history and continue to do so into these so called 'enlightened times.'

Some act occurs against one country, and that country labels that act as being evil yet the perpetrating country labels the very same act as good. Who is right and who is wrong? The collective egos of the respective countries provide their own definition. One thing for sure, it is not God, the essence, on one country's side versus the Devil on the other country's side. It is very much a human ego. So to answer your question, dear student, No, there is no devil and there is no bad and no good. They are all illusions created out of our human egos. It is our ego that gives us the interpretations and labels of good or bad.

Strive to do what is in keeping with the essence, the real you, the ego-less you, without selfish manipulations. You will find your actions will be by coincidence 'good'. Whereupon Fabious burst out laughing at the apparent contradiction. Fabious laughter was infectious and made us all burst out laughing, as we often did in the community. *After we had all calmed down, he led us into a meditation and then closed the evening.*

A chance discussion during the day lead to a student asking one night, **"How do all these positive thinking, creative visualization, Wicca, magic ceremonies and rituals and suchlike, actually work? In fact, do they work?"**

Fabious smiled and said, "Yes, they do work to a greater or lesser degree and that degree depends on the level of consciousness of whoever is applying those principles. Firstly, dear students, the thing to remember is this: if we can be completely ego-less and if we are merely the vehicles of the essence, then we would not need any of these disciplines at all. Everything that needs to happen would happen in perfect synchronicity and spontaneity. Unfortunately we are not ego-less yet.

All these methods mentioned are tools, anchors, or focussing mechanisms. They do not have some secret power in of themselves, but they can be used to focus the God-like part of us - our true essence. We literally invoke our innate power to manifest the changes we require. We can use them to by-pass all the doubts, fears, insecurities, lack of belief, lack of self worth, etc. that we have locked in our ego-selves. By doing so we enable the essence to flow through and manipulate the illusion of reality to create what is in effect *yet another illusion*, but one that we desire more consciously, as it were.

To re-cap:-

1) The essence that we truly are can manifest anything it wants.
2) Our ego gets in the way of this ability.

3) These different methods are nothing more than a ruse, designed to put our ego 'on-hold' temporarily, or in other words to suspend disbelief for periods of time. They do this by using magic rituals, or vision boards, or repeating affirmations or writing goals, visualizing and so forth.

4) While our doubt-filled ego mind is on hold, the true essence can get on with the creation process; which it is so good at."

Fabious leaned back in his chair. "I should mention, students, applying these principals and methods, gets easier and stronger and more effective as you work on decreasing your ego. You then manifest more and more of the essence through your body and daily lives. With that comes more responsibility for making sure that whatever you wish to manifest is for the greatest good because the karmic back lash can be lethal!" Fabious took a sip of his water and said, "Since that was relatively short and easy to answer students and we have some time, are there any more topics any one wishes to discuss tonight?"

A student stood up and asked, **"Astrology, Numerology, and such like, do they work and if so how?"** Fabious said; "Yes, astrology and numerology and such, do have influences in our lives. It would also be true to say that the less evolved a person is, the greater the influence. When we incarnate as I have mentioned, we incarnate with specific lessons to learn. We choose the hour of our birth, our names, the place we will incarnate, and our parents. We choose these influences to set up the conditions that will best enable us to learn the lessons we have chosen to learn this time around.

Some people live their whole lives un-conscious of their spiritual nature. They think that when they die, that is it. They have no awareness that they are part of the essence, they have no understanding that their beliefs lead on to create their experience of life on Earth. Star signs and numerology, in particular, influence these people because it is these influences that set them up for their lessons. Once, however, you start to grow in spiritual awareness the influences of external signs start to fall away as self-responsibility comes more to the fore in your lives. Ultimately the star signs set up a pattern but you can overcome any pattern with deeper awareness. Ultimately we have to grow through and into all the positive aspects of all the star signs as we re-incarnate life after life.

So, dear student, by all means study if you wish to, astrology, numerology or anything else but always remember the real you, the higher self you is above all of these things and that they really are only influences on the lower self 'you'. You have all progressed to a certain point already; otherwise you would never have been invited to this house. Now you are fast overcoming these influences and predisposing effects and moving towards taking total responsibility for everything in your life."

A student asked with much curiosity, **"Is it possible that we in this room will reach a point in time in this lifetime, where our ego is gone and God the essence, our true nature, expresses itself directly through the vehicle of our body?"** Fabious looked around the room and there was sadness in his eyes. "You ask if this is possible," said Fabious. "Yes, it is possible, that, at any point of time and at any instant, if we reach a point when our ego, our mind, ceases to exist, then all that would be left is God, the essence, flowing through our human body.

Yes, it is possible and that is good news. The other good news is that it definitely will happen at some point in time. Perhaps not in this lifetime; perhaps in one hundred lifetimes from now. It is the destiny of all of us to make this journey. Until that happens there is one thing I would advise you to do every day. It will fill you up with joy, amazement, confidence, resolve and strength, every day of your life.

So listen up," chuckled Fabious. I laughed to myself; he really didn't need to say that for there was keen interest in the body language of all the students. Fabious continued, "Just when anyone will become enlightened – filled with light – is anyone's guess, it can happen at any time. The truth of the matter is we are incarnated in a human body so we still have lessons to learn and wherever we are right now; we are in the perfect place to learn those lessons. Let enlightenment come when it will and meantime, just prove God, the essence." Fabious looked at our blank faces and listened to the dulled, puzzled silence. He smiled and took a deep breath.

"W*e may, or may not, know God, the essence, directly, in this lifetime. However, we can prove God each and every day, and in each and every moment.* Concentrate on that, and let that be your goal. Enlightenment will look after itself. Dear students, if you prove God, the essence, in all you do, your days will be full of joy and miracle will follow miracle. Coincidences will fill your lives and you will perceive the connections behind the dance we call life.

Strive to live not for the ego for it is the ego that attributes meaning to all that happens to us, and it is our ego that keeps us in bondage and darkness and away from the light. Once you learn to live life not from the ego-ruled perspective then you will sense the hidden hand of God, the essence, behind all things. As you sense this, it will speed you, feed you, fuel you and empower you to continue up the final steep and hard climb to the top of the mountain."

Fabious looked around the room at the gathered students and the love and compassion, pouring from him was palpable. It felt to me like a tide of pure energy, pulsing and bathing us all in its light.

Fabious straightened in his chair and said, "Remember these things dear students.

1) The essence, that you can call God, is everywhere; it always has been and always will be. It exists in all dimensions, all time and all space; it encompasses all that is or ever will be.
2) The essence is aware.
3) Our true inner self is that essence also.
4) Our true inner self has all the awareness the essence has.
5) The essence and the essence, which is our true selves, is one and the same energy. The essence has nothing that it has to do. It has nowhere it has to go; for it is everywhere and encompasses everything already.
6) Because we are in our true form, the essence we are already enlightened, now, so it is not actually something outside of ourselves that we have to chase or indeed can chase.
7) If you are not really aware of this, then it is your ego that has moved away from God, the essence. The essence of God has not moved away from you.
8) Our ego has created this separation and it is our ego that has created a false inner map of reality. This map we each have inside of ourselves is our own individualised ego-based interpretation of how things are and it is the ultimate illusion. However because we are, in our deepest part, the essence, with all its creative powers, we subconsciously create our individual reality and perceptions of this world to conform to that illusionary map. We mistakenly believe this map to be true.
9) The way to dissolve this false map is to systematically dismantle our egos.

10) Meditation is one powerful way of slowing the mind-ego down so you can become aware of your ego in action. You become a witness to your own thoughts, emotions, words and actions. You watch yourself happy, angry and sad. By being a witness to yourself you realise that you are an actor playing a role of being angry, sad, happy or any number of experiences. You learn you are the actor and not the role itself, whereas normally you think you are the role and therefore feel powerless to change it. You eventually realise you can have any map you want; it becomes a conscious choice.
11) As you become skilled at being the witness, your ego will dismantle and fall away naturally.
12) As it falls away more and more of the essence will shine through you and so you will start to prove God by the changes you see happening in your life. You will live more and more by intuition – inner tuition - and you will find yourself in the right place at the right time and what would seem like miracles to you now will become common place.
13) It has been said, "Be still and know you are God the essence". This means still the mind, the ego. Witness the lower self and all its lower self-ego driven ways and you will know that the essence and your true self, are one and the same."

With that Fabious stood and approached each one of us and hugged us all individually. While he was doing this I felt a sudden sinking feeling in my stomach. It was unusual for Fabious to finish one of his talks in this manner and I thought I sensed a feeling of finality in his hugs, like when a friend is giving you a hug before they set out on a long voyage somewhere. There is a strange mix of happiness slightly tinged with sadness. After Fabious had finished hugging everyone in the room he walked back to his seat. He sat quietly for a moment taking the time to look around the room into the eyes of each student there gathered.

Fabious smiled and said, "My friends the time that we have shared together has been very special to me, and I hope, special to you as well." At that point I intuitively realised what my stomach was feeling was going to be confirmed with Fabious's next words. "As I have taught over the years there is season for all things and all things happen in cycles. There is a time of starting and a time of ending. Our time together gathered here has come to a close. This time has come to an end and you and I must go onto our next beginnings and adventures," Fabious paused.

The silence in the room was deafening as the understanding of his words dawned on us all that our time with Fabious was at its end. A student with tears in her eyes asked "But why Fabious? Why must we end our learning in this place and with you? She was brave enough to ask the question that so many in the room wanted to ask. Fabious with kind eyes, smiled and said, "There is an old saying 'If you feed a hungry man fish today he will be hungry tomorrow but if you teach him to fish he never need go hungry again.' I have taught you to fish and there comes a time when you must fish for yourselves, for it is in the fishing itself that you will learn your best lessons."

Fabious continued, "A parent helps a child to grow, develop and mature but there comes a time when that parent must let go and let their child go into the world to tread its own path. This time has come. "If I was to keep you close to me forever, and not let you go then I am not your friend. I would be stunting your growth; I would be very selfish to do such a thing. All of you here gathered, are ready for your next adventure, ready to go out and carry on the lessons you have learnt here with me. You are ready to keep growing and to pass on these lessons to as many fellow souls who will listen and will hear your message."

Fabious smiled and said, "I see some long faces here, but we will not have them here tonight. Remember dear students, now is not the time to be sad for what was, but rather it is the time to be happy for what was." Fabious stood at these last words and said, "This time has come to an end, my dear students, do not moan its passing but celebrate that it was. I love you all."

Then he turned and walked out of the common room. I went to bed that night feeling a little sad that my eyes would not see Fabious again. But I also felt energized and uplifted as if a large piece of a puzzle had fallen into place inside myself, although, in truth, I could not say exactly what it was. *With deep sadness, dear reader, I must tell you that that night was the last time I ever saw Fabious.*

Bridge to Part Three

Many, many years have passed since the period I spent living with Fabious. My fellow students separated and followed their different paths in life. I am still in communication with some of the friends I made while at Fabious's house.

That each of us is radically different after our experience with Fabious cannot be denied. I would like to think that I, and my fellow students, have continued to walk the path up the mountain each in our own way.

To say that my time since Fabious has been all 'roses and no thorns' would be a lie. It is true to say, however, that by striving to live for the most part, in accordance with the teachings of Fabious, I have manifested many more roses and certainly many less thorns in my life.

So, with humility, the following section of the book is my own account of how I try to live by the teachings of Fabious and the wisdom acquired along my life's path.

It is my heartfelt hope that by passing this information on to you, it will in some way help you in your own individual journey up to the top of the mountain and that one day I will see you there.

As for Fabious, I like to think that somewhere in this world, he is teaching yet another group of students in his fashion and living and laughing just as he always was.

The Art of Consciously Living Longer

Part Three

Alternative titles that this part of the book could have had are: -

So you want to live forever?

Growing younger, being younger, staying young longer!

Anti Aging - Why not?

Growing old – is such a drag! Why bother?

Youthing with grace and vigour.

Growing old is a myth.

No Thanks – I prefer to stay young!

Staying young – longer.

All of these words could be applicable to this section.

One of the things to learn in life is that nothing happens by accident so if this book has attracted you then be assured your inner guidance has already started you moving in the direction of these teachings.

We now move to part three and part three, as mentioned previously, is divided into seven sections.

The Seven Sections are as follows: -

Overview - This is my own personal 'understanding' on spirituality. How we create our world by our thoughts, actions, beliefs and spoken word.

Yoga Techniques - These bring balance to the energy system of our body that 'Youth' us and should be practiced daily.

Mental -The right mental attitude is essential to staying young and achieving your goals.

Physical – The minimum physical practices you need to do, to remain young and vital.

Nutritional – The simple nutritional rules you should follow to provide the body the tools it needs to heal itself and stay young.

Meditation – Meditation techniques that keep your mind in balance and at peace. This enables you to hear the 'still small inner voice' within, that is the higher self you. You will learn that by doing this you will have less stress in your life and less stress means you will live longer. I will cover how traditional meditation can now be enhanced by new western technology.

The Way of the Inner Warrior – How to resolve emotional conflicts that age us and negatively affect our lives.

Overview

It is vitally important, if this section of the book is to work best for you that you have an understanding of just how powerful you are as a creature of the universe....

...How you have more control over what happens to you in your life than you realise, and much more than you take credit or responsibility for.

This understanding is necessary as you progress through this part of the book because many of the following sections stem from these basic belief systems and truisms.

'How Things Are'

Essentially, we are all made from the primal God stuff; which I often refer to as 'The Essence.' Try not to get hung up on the 'God' word. It doesn't matter what you call it. The point is, what we think we are and what we 'actually' are, are quite different. Over many lifetimes we have built a shell around our true nature. This shell I call our ego or lower self. We have identified with it and have come to believe it is what we are. This ego self, or lower self, interprets the world through tinted glasses and perceives things as being separate from us. It sees other people as different; it sees things in terms of 'this is mine' and 'that is not mine.' It creates an 'us and them' situation, 'winners and losers', 'I am right, they are wrong' feelings. It buys into what a particular society teaches without thinking for itself or challenging the status quo.

This viewpoint in life means it is necessary to control life, the situations encountered and the people around you, to keep your *ego well fed, safe and alive. It is probably the single, biggest cause of suffering in the world generally and in our lives personally. It creates artificial boundaries; it is the part of us that believes that we have to grow old and that to be happy we need a nice car, house, the latest gizmo and such things.*

It is truly the world of illusions. We have become so involved and identified with this lower self that we have forgotten that we are truly children of God, with the potential to reclaim our heritage. An important part of 'Youthing' is to break down the mental barriers created by our ego and believe that all things are possible and what we hold and see in our inner mind is what we manifest in reality.

It means taking responsibility for whatever situation we find ourselves in right now, good or bad. By breaking down the barriers and changing our thought patterns we can manifest what we want to be.

To summarise this:

Since the basic You is a part of God, then you are like the seed from a great oak tree, and that seed has the potential to become a great oak. So, by extension, you have the untapped power of God. Your word, or will, is law for you. As you think so shall it be. The thoughts you choose to believe will manifest as your reality. If you believe that life is unfair then you will find it unfair.

If you believe you only attract the wrong partners in life, whom so ever you do attract will be 'wrong'. If you believe that money is hard to come by, then it will be. If you anticipate ill health, old age, winding down in later years, then this is exactly what will happen. **It is said, "If you think you can, you can. If you think** *you can't, you can't." Psychologists, sport coaches, personal trainers would all agree with this. Doctors know that if a patient has lost the will to live then it is usually 'lights out' time.*

So, let's think it through. If you are part of the God stuff with a God inherent unlimited power and one day while walking in the countryside you come across a creek and you think, 'I can't jump that creek'. Then you, as part of God have decreed, you cannot jump that creek. So when you fail in the attempt, you actually haven't failed at all. You have been tremendously successful in applying the rule of law i.e. 'what you will shall be the law for you.' So if, as God, you believe that it is natural to grow old, to become less agile, less focused, grow weak and die, then you are fulfilling your own prophecy with all the power of a God.

The good news is that the ties that bind us, limit us, hurt us, impair us, are as strong as gossamer threads. All you have to do is be open to the ideas I have shared with you and already you will find a change happening at a cellular level.

Watch your thoughts; guard against any negative thoughts and ideas, which sneak into your mind. Substitute positive thoughts, ideas, dreams, beliefs, actions, words and the battle is already starting to turn in your favour. The next example is just an analogy I use to explain further how I see it all happening.

The Ocean Analogy

Imagine an Ocean. It's perfect just being an ocean. Some people say, "Gee perfection must be pretty boring." But think of an ocean. It can be smooth and serene, rough and stormy, a beautiful deep blue or a soft green. It is still an ocean, but hardly boring.

Now imagine the sun beats down on the ocean and a water droplet decides for a bit of 'fun' it would be nice to be separate from the ocean for a while and ride that cloud, have an adventure. So it evaporates and rises until it reaches the cloud. At that point it knows it belongs to the ocean but is enjoying the ride on the cloud.

Now imagine after a moment in time, the cloud passes some land and the drop separates from the cloud and begins a long descent towards the ground. As it falls the exhilaration of the fall wipes out its memory of the ocean. It forgets that it is greater than a drop and that it is part of something greater than itself.

<u>A digression:</u> This is the equivalent of the birth trauma you experienced; designed to wipe out your memories of your past lives – and the truth that you are part of God on a tremendous adventure of your choosing. It is part of the total immersion into the make believe adventure you have chosen, the lessons you have chosen to learn in this lifetime.

You may ask, "Why do we have to forget?" Two main reasons: - one is so we have total immersion in this life and feel it as raw emotions, good and bad. If we did remember that it is all make believe, then we would not play the game as hard. The second reason: - let's say we have decided to learn this lifetime that it is okay to be dependant and receive help from others and so we choose to be a paraplegic. If we remembered that really, we are a free 'Being,' capable of unlimited movement we may well choose to kill ourselves rather than play the game out and learn the lessons.

Suicide by the way is a big spiritual NO –NO. It means you get on the expressway back into another body being reborn to experience the same lessons again , usually with a few extra lessons added. A bit like a naughty school boy who has to repeat the same school year, this time under the watchful eye of a hard taskmaster of a teacher.

As a side issue why is a being conceived and then aborts or miscarries? Sometimes a soul incarnates to finish its karmic implications and this can be done in the womb. Or sometimes a soul incarnates for two or three months in the womb to set up a situation whereby its parents have the opportunity to learn their lessons from the experience. All things happen for a reason and from a human perspective what seems so bad, is in fact just part of the learning we need; for ALL parties concerned.

So our droplet falls and falls and it lands on a mountaintop and for a while it is on the mountain (an adventure) then it seeps into the ground (another adventure). It hits a root and is sucked up into a plant (another adventure). An animal eats the leaf the droplet is in (another adventure). Another animal eats that animal in turn (another adventure). It passes through that animal and is urinated onto the ground (another adventure). It moves through the ground (another adventure) and is purified by the rocks (another adventure). One day it meets other drops on their adventures; they join together and become a brook (another adventure), then a stream (another adventure), then a river (another adventure). Eventually (over many many lifetimes and many such adventures), it rejoins the ocean and in so doing remembers what it was, what it is and what it always will be.

This is the journey of our essential self. It is important to realise that you are like that drop of water, lost in many adventures over many lifetimes, until, at last, like the little droplet, you, too, return to your true essential self. It is an important step to realise that aging, ill

health, etc. are all illusions, and that the essential you can change it all. It is possible to reverse aging and by cultivating the possibility in our mind, we start a process of changing ourselves, transforming ourselves into a youthful, active and vibrant being.

Five Yoga Techniques

The five yoga techniques explained at the end of this section will bring your body into alignment and create an environment in your body to begin the Youthing process. First however I will give you the background explanation on how these five yogic techniques contribute to better health.

Plan your daily routine for the rest of your life. They can be completed in as little as ten minutes a day. Ten minutes of your time in return for anti-aging is a very small price to pay.

The reason why these exercises work is:

1) *Your body lives within you not the other way round. The lower self i.e. ego, thinks it is inside the confines of the physical body. It thinks the real you is the physical body.*
2) *The real you projects out, way past the physical body. Most of us have heard of the Aura of a person, which extends out at least one metre in healthy people. This Aura is also part of the real you, so in this fashion, the physical you is only one aspect of the real you and the physical self is inside the real you.*

In our real form, we are high-speed vibratory beings. This state is the higher self-form, mentioned in previous parts of this book. It is the step below the pure essence itself. It is at the hub of the Karmic wheel. Now if this high-speed vibratory being suddenly inhabited the dense physical body, it would be too much for the body.. It would combust immediately because the density of matter is at a much lower vibratory level. Consequently there are a series of bodies that we actually have; each one, stepping down from a higher energy to a lower energy level, eventually able to animate the dense physical body safely.

It starts with the spiritual energy body which steps down to the mental body that in turn steps down to the astral body, which then steps down to the etheric body and finally we arrive at the physical body.

The car analogy

Think of it as a car engine, which is running at very high revolutions. If the power from the engine were suddenly transmitted directly to the wheels, it would cause significant damage. The drive shaft would certainly shatter, probably the crankshaft as well. It wouldn't work, simply put. So we have a clutch that merges the speed of the engine so that the wheels slowly turn at first, eventually speeding up.

The clutch in this analogy is doing the same job as the various bodies I have described, like a series of step-dow transformers. *Each of these bodies has a corresponding energy point situated in the body. These are called Chakra. Think of them as whirling balls of energy.*

There are seven main Chakras. Clairvoyants see Chakra in various colours. Each Chakra influences various organs, glands and nerve plexus in the body. They stimulate glands of the endocrine system to produce various hormones that regulate the body and its cells. They are situated in different parts of the body.

The lowest and closest to the physical plane called the first or the lower Chakra (red) is located at the perineum. This is the spot between the anus and the testicles of a male and vagina of a female. It's associated with sexual energy, physical relations between people and physicality.

The second Chakra (orange) is the social Chakra. It is found in the body three to four inches below the belly button and is associated with how we interact socially with people and the environment and our emotions.

The third Chakra (yellow) is situated where the solar plexus sits, just below where the ribs come together. This Chakra is associated with the intellect and emotion.

The fourth Chakra (green) is the heart Chakra. It is found in the middle of the chest at heart level. It is the love Chakra and influences how we interact with our feelings.

The fifth Chakra (blue) is situated in the throat. It is involved with how we express ourselves socially, intellectually, and emotionally. It enables us to put into words our psychic intuition, and helps us express our God-self nature, while on this earth.

The sixth Chakra (purple) is our psychic centre. It is found in the middle of the forehead. It has been called the third eye.

The seventh or crown Chakra (white sometimes violet tinged) is situated on the crown of the head. It connects us to our God self, via our "higher self".

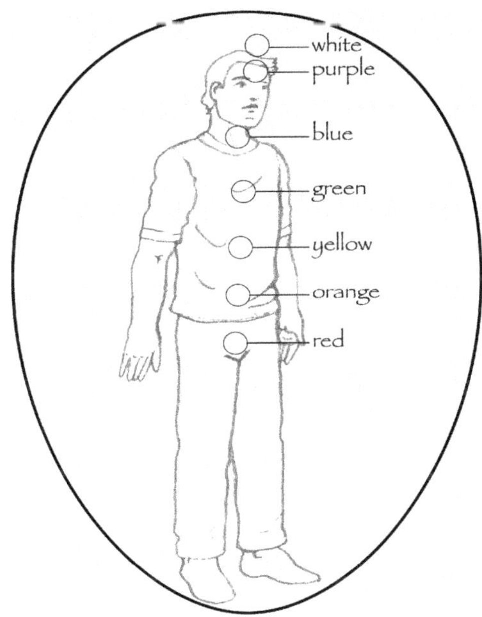

I discovered the existence of the Chakra energy system *and the* Aura *as a nine year old. I learnt to feel them as clearly as if I were to touch my nose. I discovered them by doing a very simple exercise. You may care to try it.*

Remember though you do not have to experience or feel the Chakra or Aura for the Yoga Techniques to work. Choose a quiet time when you will not be interrupted for 20 – 30 minutes.

Firstly sit upright in a comfortable chair.

Then take three deep breathes and consciously relax the body. Breathe in to your lower tummy so it rises first, and then fill up the mid chest so it rises secondly, then lastly, breath into upper chest. In other words, a full deep breathe. Hold your breath, count three full seconds and then slowly exhale fully. Repeat this two more times.

Mentally focus and place your awareness into your <u>*toes*</u> *and notice all the feelings your toes can feel. Imagine a checklist in your mind and you are ticking off all the feelings your toes are registering, as you focus on them. Examples – You may notice, if you have socks on, the feel of the material against your toes; perhaps some toes feel this pressure more than other. Note these differences. Once you have noticed and ticked off all the feelings you are aware of in your toes move onto noticing all the feelings your* <u>*feet*</u> *are registering.*

Example - The bottom of your feet you may be able to feel the pressure of the floor pressing up against them; perhaps a temperature difference between the soles of your feet and the top of your feet. Next, move to awareness of your <u>*shins and calves*</u>*. Example – if you have pants on you may be aware of the material of the pants against your skin. If you are wearing baggy pants, perhaps some part of your shins or calves won't feel that material at all. Try to become aware of any differences. If the backs of your calves are pressing against a seat base, you will be aware of that extra pressure on the calves.*

Next move your awareness to your <u>*thighs*</u> *and focus on any sensations you can experience there. Example – perhaps part or all of the back of the thigh is pressing down into the seat, maybe part of the back of the thigh is against the chair and part is free of the chair. Can you feel where the chair stops? On the front of the thigh you may feel the material of your clothing. Perhaps part of your thigh feels hotter or colder.*

Next move your awareness to your <u>buttocks</u> see what they are feeling. Examples – You can feel the weight of gravity pulling them down onto the seat. You may feel how the buttocks, are warmed by the seat etc. Next become aware of your <u>hips</u>, what are they feeling? Then your <u>lower back</u> what is that feeling? Examples – The small of your back may feel warmer as it presses into the seat. Perhaps one part of your lower back is more in contact with the seat than other parts. Can you discern any difference?

Now be aware of your <u>tummy</u> and all it feels. Example – as you breathe in can you notice a small rise and fall motion? Perhaps there is a tight feeling of clothing bunched around tummy etc. Now be aware of your <u>upper back</u>.

Examples – Does it feel warmer than your front as it is contacting the chair etc? Next is <u>chest;</u> what can you feel? Examples – Does it rise and fall with each breath; can you feel your chest moving up and down etc. Next be aware of your <u>shoulders</u>. Example - are they relaxed etc

Become aware of your <u>fingers and hands</u>. What are they feeling? Can you feel any temperature difference between the palms which may be face down against material on your thighs or tummy and the back of the hand - exposed to the air? Can you feel where some fingers may be resting against other fingers etc? Next become aware of your <u>forearms</u>.

Examples - What can you feel? Perhaps differences in pressure between the bottom of your forearms and the top? Temperature, feelings?

Now go on to your <u>upper arms.</u> Imagine your arms relaxing along with the relaxation now being experienced in your shoulders as well as the rest of your body. Now shift your awareness to your <u>neck muscles</u>. Examples – what is your neck feeling? Does it feel the headrest of the chair supporting it? Can you feel the air against your neck? Does the skin that is covered by clothing feel warmer to you? Can you be aware of the line made by the contrast of cooler skin exposed to the air, and the warmer skin under your clothes?

Now be aware of the <u>scalp.</u> Allow it to relax, and then finally the <u>facial muscles</u> - let them relax in the same way being aware of any feelings experienced. You will be significantly more relaxed by now than when you began the exercise. You will find that as your awareness moves into the different parts of your body, that part will automatically start to relax. <u>Side note:</u> This exercise works extremely well at night when lying in bed. You simply follow the same procedure and chances are you will fall asleep before you get through the entire body, so please remember and apply it. Good sleep is important for anti – aging.

Take about 10 – 15 minutes to work through the body in this fashion. Now take your hands and rub them together for 10 seconds in a circular motion and then separate them so they are about 25 to 50 mm (one to two inches) apart.

Keep looking at the gap between your hands. It is very important that you keep your hands moving in small circles. You will only feel Chakra and Auras when your energy field moves through them. Notice any feelings your hands begin to feel. It seems to be different for different people. Some feel hot or cold only, some tingling feelings, pins and needle feelings, others, myself included, feel a strong magnetic feeling like two north ends of a magnet being pushed together.

As you begin to feel some feelings, slowly, keeping your hands moving in gentle circles, move your hands apart. You will find you can feel that same feeling even as your hands move further apart, 600mm to 900mm (2 – 3 feet) even more. What you are now feeling is your Aura. You may wish to feel what the Chakra actually feels like. Simply have a friend lay down on the floor on their back. Tune in your hands first, as described above. Once you have done that, move a hand (I use my right hand) slowly over the person's body, about a foot away, making sure you keep the hands moving in those small circles.

As you pass each Chakra you will feel that extra magnetic feeling or warm or cold feeling which you felt when you were tuning into your own Aura. With practice it becomes easier and automatic and you will be able to tell if someone is out of balance in his or her system quite easily. Ideally we should have the Chakra all in balance and of the same size and strength.

This is for two reasons. The first is so we have a balanced personality; enjoying the ability to live healthily in all seven planes here on Earth: physically, socially, mentally, emotionally with love and feelings, and able to express all these attributes, to experience psychic abilities and pure spirituality. The second reason has to do with anti aging, the main topic of this section. The Chakra affects different organs in the body as well as the endocrine system, which produces hormones that regulate bodily functions.

When the Chakra are all spinning in balance and in unison, we have perfect health and 'Youthing.' The goal of these five Yoga exercises is to stimulate the Chakra and bring them all into balance with each other. Some of these exercises influence more than one Chakra. Please remember if you did not feel the Aura in the above exercise it really doesn't matter. It is not even essential that you believe in the Chakra or Aura.

The yoga techniques will work in any case.

So let's get on with the techniques!

Five Anti-Aging Yoga Techniques

Note:

1) *Start out doing just a few repetitions of each of the positions, depending on your current health and fitness level. Do NOT strain yourself in any way.*
2) *The goal is to eventually build up to doing 21 repetitions of each position.*
3) *Do the techniques daily; they can be done in 10 minutes.*
4) *If in doubt check with your doctor before starting the techniques.*
5) *There is no rush to get to 21, start gradually and build up slowly.*
6) *Consistency is more important than quantity and speed.*

First Technique - Spinning

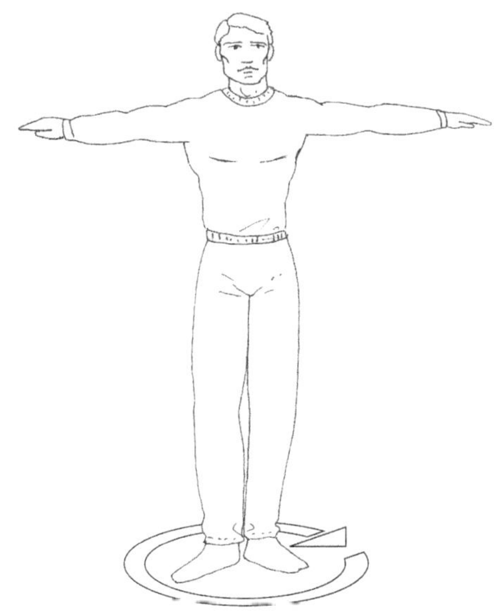

Stand straight then slowly begin spinning on the spot. Always in a clockwise, left to right direction. Arms straight out, horizontal to body so blood moves down arms towards hands. One rotation is completed, when you have spun round and facing where you started. Go at a speed you are comfortable with. Always go in the same direction clockwise.

Second Technique – Leg Raisers

Lay flat on the floor on your back. Legs together. Now at same time – breathe in and raise your head so that your chin goes to your chest while at same time raising your legs, to a vertical position then breathe out lowering your head and legs to the floor. This is one count. At first you may have to bend your legs as you lift, but over time it will become easier and easier.

Third Technique- Back Arches

Kneel on the floor, in an upright stance, with your hands resting on your lower back. Firstly, breathe out and as you do so, lower your chin to your chest. Secondly, as you breathe in, tilt your head back as far as is comfortable and arching backwards, hold for a second or two then breathe out.

As you do so bring your head forward to rest on your chest, which is the starting position. This is one count.

Fourth Technique- Table Top

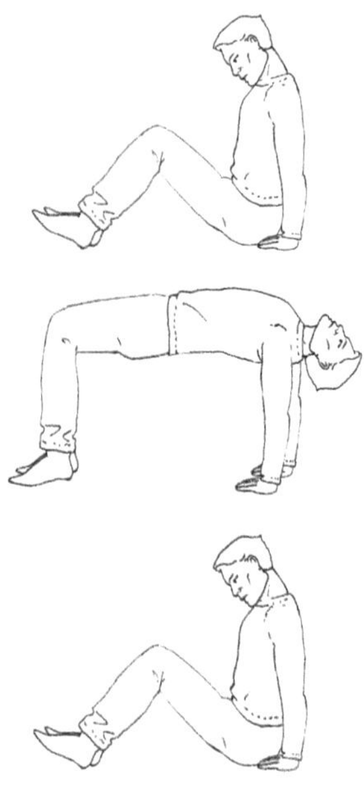

Start sitting on floor, feet comfortably apart and bent legs so your heels are flat on floor. Your arms are straight down with your hands placed on the floor beside your hips. Two stages. As you breathe out lower your chin to your chest, then while inhaling lift your body upwards so that your back is horizontal with the floor - you create a tabletop, as it were. Tilt your head back as far as it will comfortably go. Hold this position for one or two seconds then breathe out lowering your buttocks to start position with your chin resting on chest. This is one count.

Fifth Technique- The Bow

Start by laying flat on the floor on your stomach, legs approximately a shoulder width apart, with toes curled so balls of feet can take some of your weight. This technique is in two parts. Firstly just press up, straightening your arms to full extension letting your back sag so hips are still close to floor at same time breathe out and tilt head back as far as comfortable. Part two.

While breathing in lift your buttocks straight up into the bringing your body into an “inverted V” position. Keep your chin tucked in towards your chest so you see your feet –then breathe out and lower your buttocks back to the start position. Your arms are straight through the whole exercise; it is not a western type press up. This is one count.

So these are the five Yoga Techniques.

Do them daily, starting with only as many as you can comfortably do, building up over time to 21 repetitions of each position.

I challenge you *to do them for 3 months every day and within 3 months you will notice tremendous changes taking place within your body.*

Footnote: - The spinning technique reminds me of the superb Whirling dervishes of Turkey and their spinning spiritual technique, a remarkably robust group of people. The other techniques and multiple variations have been taught in the schools of Hatha Yoga for centuries. For more detail on these I would recommend a book called “Ancient secret of the fountain of youth” by Peter Kelder

The <u>Mental</u> Aspect For Youthing

For longevity we have to change the way we think. Or more correctly: - think correctly. Once you understand the "Essential You" is really the God in you, you will understand that the "God Stuff" can manifest into your life whatever you desire; if it is in alignment with what you need in this life time, in order to fulfil your lessons or divine plan. This applies equally to material possessions and wealth, relationships and the physical body. The physical body, I believe is the most important, followed by relationships and material wealth. I am sure at the time of writing this there are millionaires, somewhere in the world, on their deathbeds, who would give all their money away just to have great health again.

In other words, the inner you has the power to change and manifest in the physical body that which you hold to be true in your inner mind. You must guard your mind in what it thinks about yourself and you must, even more so, guard your tongue and the words you say about yourself. For what you say and think about yourself consistently will be what you bring into reality.

When you hold a picture of yourself in your mind's eye of youthfulness and vitality and you speak only words that reflect that attitude, then truly *you are hastening the ability of your body to bring about Youthing and longevity. It all starts in the mind. All you need is a 'crack in the door' to the possibility that all I have said is true and correct and you have started the process.* All that remains, then, is for you to prove the efficacy of this anti-aging process by adopting the lifestyle changes found within this book. The results will speak for themselves and that crack will open wider and wider until the door is ripped off its hinges and the way for startling changes in your life is fully opened. There is a common saying, "your thoughts create reality" I agree with this 100 per cent. Numerous studies have confirmed that optimistic people tend to attract more than their fair share of positive experiences and generally are healthier and live longer than pessimists. Why is that? It is simply because the spiritual law is in motion. It is not rocket science, that's for sure. This concept has been taught in 'Mystery Schools' throughout man's history as a secret of discipleship. However the western mind requires proof before it can be open to new possibilities. It is in the realm of Quantum Physics that science is proving our thoughts literally do create our realities.

In a nutshell, Quantum Physicists study increasingly smaller packets of matter as technology improves. They have been able to measure and observe increasingly smaller particles. At one time the atom was thought to be the smallest unit of matter. However, as smaller particles of matter were discovered, it was noticed that they had some very interesting qualities. The most important one being, these smaller packets of matter behaved in ways the observer expected or 'willed' them to behave, to the point of even appearing in two places at once and at the same time! This is known as the 'observer effect'.

I don't profess to understand the science of how this could be so, I will leave that to the scientists. If however, the building blocks of matter form up in ways that meet the expectations of the observer, we had all better learn to control our thoughts; for they do in turn go on to create our realities. For those that want more information on this aspect a good video to watch is "What the bleep do we know!"

We come next to an understanding of what I call "The Three Aspects Of Man". Man in this context refers to men and women equally. The three aspects can be conceptualised as follows:-

Lower self

Higher self

Doorway to our true inner core

At our centre is what I call "The Door way to our Inner True Core." Beyond this doorway is the real us. It is the essential God stuff. It is truly who we are. We are on this level - God. All of us equal, as God encompasses everything and there is nothing outside of God for God is in everything and everything is in God. It is the part that knows all, knows the divine plan of why we came here and what we choose to experience this lifetime. It knows the lessons we came here to learn this time.

It is an infinite powerhouse of energy and vibration. It is the level where anything is possible and from which all things manifest. It is the unlimited potential. It is the powerhouse behind all miracles and it is the springboard that creates all we experience and the source of all we will experience in our future. It always was, always is and always will be. It is the only absolute. It is beyond time and space for they are illusions of our ego's perception. It actually has nothing it has to do, nowhere it has to go, it is everywhere and nowhere, it is the physical made manifest and it is the as yet, un-manifested. Call this powerhouse whatever you like: God, Buddha, Universal Love, Ram, Subconscious Mind etc.

This part is just waiting for our lower ego self to get out of the way and to wake up and reclaim our heritage. This is the choice humans have. It is the free will spoken about. No one else can make that choice for us. The main lesson we are all here to learn is we have a choice and we can choose to manifest into our life, all the good we can picture in our mind's eye and all that is in line with our divine plan. Surrounding the door to our true inner core powerhouse is what I call our "Higher Self."

This is, I stress, still ego based. It is one step if you like, separated from the inner core. Ultimately it is an illusion for it is not the absolute, which remember, is the only non-illusion. It is an aspect of us that can exist outside of the physical body and it can reincarnate time and time again over many lifetimes. At the higher self's end of its journey lays the ultimate sacrifice, for eventually it must cease to be. It is aware of this as well. It chooses and knows the wisdom of letting the powerhouse that is our essential self, rule our lives. It acts as a channel onto this plane of the ultimate energy source. It is the part of us that always acts in our best interests and in the best interests of all other beings we encounter in our life. It co-creates our lives on this plane in conjunction with the powerhouse inside our core. It is the source of our conscious and the still small voice within; known as our intuition.

Surrounding the higher self and therefore also surrounding our door to the true inner core as well, is our "Lower Self" ego. This is the aspect that most of us are aware of and we live out of, most of the time, often mistakenly believing it is whom we really are. For most of us we have no concept of our inner core and perhaps only fleeting glimpses of our higher self. This is the part of us that thinks we have to be in control of all aspects of our lives.

It is the part that creates all our problems and hassles in life. It totally drops away when we leave our current body and ceases to be the moment we pass on; for it never really was. It is that part of us that colours our reality to conform to what we expect life to be like and what we expect life to deliver to us, mostly based on our past experiences.

This lower self has been ignoring the true essential self, our higher self, and has been going it alone, trying to keep control for years and years. It has sent orders to the inner self of how it wants our world to be and like a good servant the higher self via the powerhouse within, has been doing its best to create a world that fits the misconceptions of the lower self. The lower self is the face that we show to the world. It has its good points but also holds hidden doubts, fears, and belief in lack, poverty, ill health, aging and the eventual death of the physical body. The trick of the game we call life is to break out of the crust of our lower ego.

We need to see it as it really is, an illusion, and learn to feel and act out of our higher self-ego awareness; ultimately becoming an expression of the inner core directly into this plane. The question is how to start? It is easier than you think. If you have read this far and understand the ideas we have covered then the process is starting to happen already. As you read, your mind becomes open to new possibilities. The lower self will, most likely, for most of us, be there ready to bring forth all negative thoughts and conditions possible, whenever it can. So we need to side step it completely.

The medium to do this, the secret, is in our **spoken word**. The power of what we say to ourselves when alone and to others, when in company. This is the key; this is the secret Rosetta stone, this is the 'Re-Educator' and the changer. It is our spoken word that will activate the essential self and finally release the inner powerhouse so it will manifest into our lives that which is best for us.

It is our birthright to experience perfect health, youthfulness, vitality, fulfilling relationships, and prosperity as well as to achieve the lessons that we have chosen for ourselves in this lifetime, i.e. perfect self-expression. Get into the habit from this moment onwards of watching every word that comes out of your mouth because by your words you will manifest. As an example: - There are people who say, "I am always unlucky" or they say, "I should be so lucky." Well surprise, surprise, they have an abundance of unlucky experiences.

Yet others say "I am so lucky" or "I am always pretty lucky" and you guessed it, they seem to be. So what words do you often say? Now you have to take it one step further and consciously start saying words to yourself relating to the things you want to happen in your life.

Some examples could be:-

"All good things come to me, I have perfect health, perfect wealth, a perfect relationship and perfect work. It has all come to me in perfect ways for the good of all concerned."

"I am feeling younger and more vital with more energy every day, miracles happen in wondrous ways for the good of all concerned."

"I stand aside and watch the divine plan of my life manifest in my affairs. In ways that benefit all concerned"

"Each day I feel younger than the day before: - healthier and more vital, miracles happen for the best for all concerned."

Some rules:-

I repeat statements like this either out loud when alone or to myself if in company as I don't want the men in white coats dragging me off! I always add, "For the greatest good for all concerned" or words to that effect, as I don't want some situation to come about for me at the expense of someone else. Doing so can incur karmic backlash; something you definitely want to avoid.

It is best to write your own wording, keep it relatively short, easy to remember, even a jingle of some sort. This impresses the powerhouse inside us more, it seems. Clean up your day-to-day wording, watch what comes out of your mouth, if you hear yourself saying anything negative, immediately affirm the opposite. Catching yourself like this will drive the message home to your powerhouse.

Become more aware of what other people say about themselves and how they literally talk themselves into trouble by their words. It is amazing once you know what to look for, how obvious this all becomes.

Remember, whatever the situations currently existing in your life that you are not happy with, you have created them by your words and actions. This may be the result of negative thinking over many years. While it is possible to change instantly and indeed I have seen instant changes in my life experiences, as often as not, it can take time to overcome years of negative thought processes. It is in fact a process, and there is no time like the present to begin..

Once it starts to happen the good news is that it increases in speed exponentially and changes follow changes faster and faster; but you must get the ball rolling first until it becomes a habit. Perseverance is the key. The other important aspect is to act as if whatever you wish to manifest into your life has already arrived. It is here now; it just hasn't become concrete yet. You have to act however, as if it has. The reason for this is that by acting as if it has already arrived, you will begin to feel as if it has. Having the feel of it in your being and your emotions is the quickest and surest way of activating the God power inside to release it to you.

I really have to emphasis this vital point. Many people have read or know of the power of positive affirmations. However a lot of these people will say the words, repeating them often, so intellectually they think they are doing the right thing to change the subconscious negative programming, but they are forgetting an important aspect.

The subconscious is a feeling entity. It is not an intellectual process. If it were none of us would have any problems as adults. The subconscious is a feeling beast as it were. The only sure way to counter years of negative thought processes is by invoking affirmations and visualisations that make us feel in our body the very changes we want to manifest as if they have happened already.

If you are doing any sort of creative visualisation and positive affirmations is it vitally important that you feel as if you have achieved your goal, target, and aspiration. If that feeling is absent you must be creative and think of new affirmations that engender this feeling. The other important step is to train yourself at all times **to act** as if you have already obtained your goal. As an example, if you wish to have more prosperity then you must act as if you did.. Pay your bills with joy and without fear, don't skimp on meals, act in a prosperous way and become prosperous.

Now how does that relate to anti-aging specifically? Well firstly you have to be open to the possibility that indeed anything is possible, including anti-aging and that it starts in the mind. I hope by what you have read so far in this book you have achieved that "open minded" feeling. Secondly by understanding how important it is to act as if a goal (in this case anti-aging) is already achieved.

If you study how a confident young person walks, you will notice they walk tall and straight, with their chest out and stomach in keeping their head up in a proud manner. The saying "ten foot tall and bullet proof" comes to mind. It follows that from now on you must consciously start to walk in this fashion. You will be amazed just by doing this alone how it will change people's perception of you and when you add all the other aspects discussed so far, to this simple exercise, you are well on your way to Youthing.

The Physical Aspect

This chapter covers the minimum physical practices you need to do to remain young and vital. It is important to remember that the "goal" is to increase life and the vitality within that life; it is not about having a body like Mr or Mrs Universe. Doing any sort of exercise is odorous and onerous to the average Joe at best, and if you are like me, to be avoided if humanly possible.

There are so many experts in the physical exercise world and I am sure they are all right in what they say we need to do, to keep fit and be well. However for the average Joe and Josephine, they expect so much that it is almost predetermined failure will eventuate.

I must have joined different gyms at least three times in my life and after a few weeks given up, as the strain was just too much. The pain simply wasn't worth the gain. How many of you have done that also? It is important to keep it simple.

Start where you are now and slowly increase to build up to the minimum I will describe.

As part of anti aging it cannot be denied, if you are fitter and not carrying round too much extra padding you will live longer.

So now a decision to bite the bullet and take your medicine, as it were, has to be reached. When you realise you are adding years to your life and life to your years it really is worth it.

The trick now is to work out the minimum requirements that will achieve results for the shortest amount of time and inconvenience.

I will firstly describe below, what the target is that you need to build up to.

Target

3 times per week with a day's rest in-between, combine weight resistance exercise, with some type of aerobic exercise.

The first 25 minutes is weight resistance training with low weights and high repetitions. After this, finish with 20 minutes of aerobic exercise such as running, swimming or if you go to a gym, 20 minutes on the cross trainer, tread mill, rowing machine, bike etc.

You can substitute one of these sessions with a 40 minute run if you prefer.

That's it in a nutshell.

My Suggestion:

I had no desire to look like Mr Universe so I went to a personal trainer at a gym. I asked her to work out a 25-minute workout, using dumb bells, as these are easy to use at a gym or to buy a cheap home set. I only wanted to work on chest, biceps, triceps, back and shoulder muscles, I told her. I figured the running would look after my legs.

She wanted to go into a full exercise routine so I had to be politely forceful. She worked out a simple set of exercises with low weights and higher repetitions, which is good for toning muscles. Is it the best exercise programme in the world? Maybe not, but if you do it religiously three times a week you will be amazed how you feel and look after even a few months. I started on small weights that were easy to lift, and worked slowly up, so that it was a little strain but not an intense one. Now it is just a matter of adding a bit more weight, to keep that slight strain feeling.

As always consult your doctor if in doubt about taking on any exercise programme. The following is the weight routine I use and is included as an example. You may like to adopt this or parts of it to create your own programme.

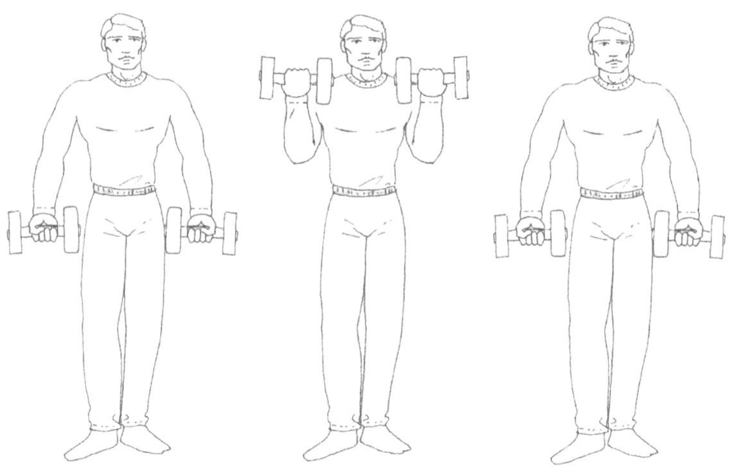

Dumbbell Bicep Curls.

Do 2 sets consisting of 15 repetitions in each set.

Dumbbell Tricep Overhead Extension

Do 2 sets consisting of 15 repetitions in each set. Do two arms at same time.

Dumbbell Shoulder Press

Do 2 sets consisting of 15 repetitions in each set.

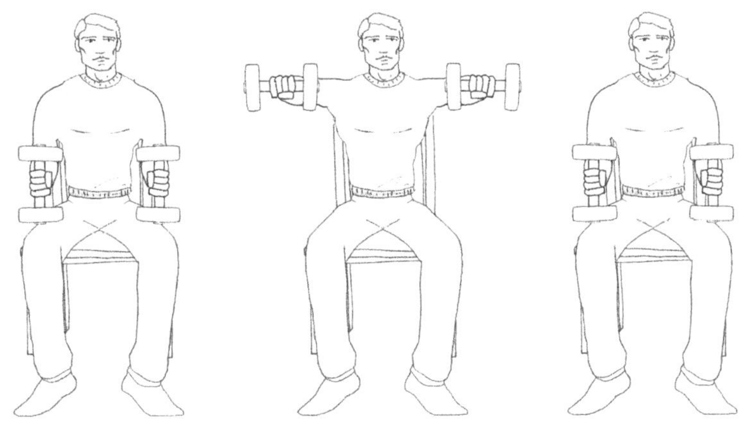

Dumbbell Shoulder Side Raise

Do 2 sets consisting of 15 repetitions in each set.

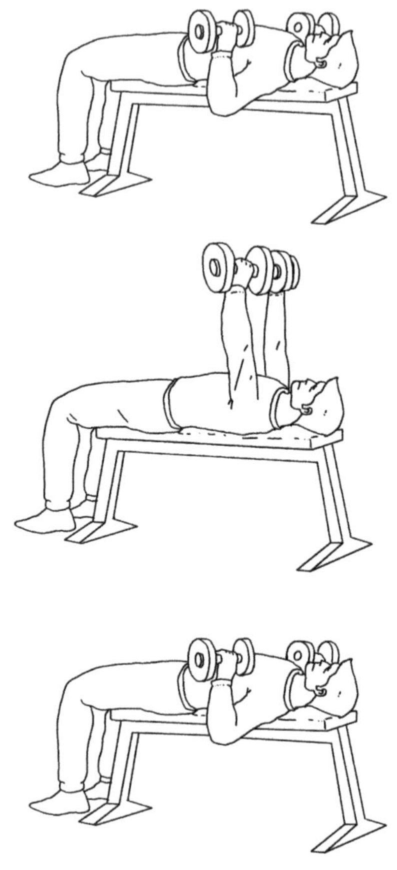

Dumbbell Shoulder Side Raise

Do 2 sets consisting of 15 repetitions in each set.

Dumbbell Bent Over Row

Do 2 sets consisting of 15 repetitions in each set.

Please remember, use small weights that only strain a little, adding more over time when comfortable. Rest between sets until comfortable to do the next set. I assume, like me, a lot of people reading this will find the above a bit too much for them in the early stages. Remember a journey of any type starts with the first footstep. It is important to get the body moving. An old saying "Use it or lose it" springs to mind here. If initially you find the above routines too difficult then forget the weight resistance temporarily and start out by going for 3 X 20 minutes walks per week. As you feel able to, on these walks, run for one lamppost and then walk for 5 lampposts, repeating this until you slowly run for more lampposts building up to running for the whole 20 minutes. Once you can do that, add an additional 25 minutes of walking until you can run for 45 minutes without stopping. When you have achieved this, you are most likely ready to do the 25-minute weight resistance routine followed by 20-minute aerobic workout. Remember, Rome wasn't built in a day. You are doing this for yourself so it is the journey to Youthing that is the goal and the adventure and you are not competing with anyone else.

Keep in mind two facts:

1) As you build up a little more muscle mass, your body will burn more calories, even when you sleep or are sitting down. This helps you keep trim and fitter more easily.
2) Resistance training, even with light weights will result in your bones becoming stronger and therefore less prone to breaks. This has been proven even in 60 – 70 years olds. You are never too old to start your journey towards Youthing.

While on the Physical side of things it should be mentioned that most likely, we all have bad habits that we know we need to change. Try to identify those in your own lifestyle and have a goal to eliminate them, one at a time.

DRUGS

Illicit drugs

Illicit drugs like Heroin, Cocaine, LSD, and Marijuana etc, forget them. They wear down the body; but worse they wear down the essential part of yourself or more correctly they create a barrier between your lower ego self and the God-like part in you that can enable you to look and feel more youthful and attract more prosperity, positive relationships, intuition and miracles into your life, on a daily basis.

Alcohol

Alcohol is not that good for you either. Though red wine has had some good reports associated with it interestingly enough. However, I doubt the average Joe or Josephine will be prepared to give it up entirely. In addition you do want some fun in the longer life you will lead. So stick to the rule of having small amounts while social drinking with friends. The camaraderie experienced in good vibes and good social interacting will probably outweigh any negative effects of the drink consumed. A rule I have is " I never drink alone". I only drink in social situations. This also means I am a cheap date as a small amount goes a long way with me.

Tobacco

Almost don't have to write anything here. However it would be negligent of me, to not say, it is best to give it up. So many studies have been done that it is patently obvious smoking is prematurely aging.

Medical drugs

While I accept that some conditions do require medical prescription drugs, I also believe that if you are in tune with your inner self and living the divine plan you came in to achieve, and then you will not need these types of drugs either. I feel that by adopting the right habits, as described in the seven sections in this book, you may well find your need for even medical drugs will diminish. Do, however, always consult your Doctor before reducing or stopping any medication you may currently be taking. In fact as you incorporate into your lifestyle these disciplines and training and if you are taking any medical prescriptions, I implore you to keep a close relationship with your doctor on this journey because the changes these techniques will create in your body are very powerful.

Get plenty of sleep

Sleep deprivation is a definite no-no. When I say sleep, I mean natural sleep not one that is either medical or otherwise drug related. Good natural sleep is so important to anti–aging. If you do have trouble sleeping then the following is a shortened recap/reminder of the relaxation technique from the 5 Yoga Techniques chapter.

For sleep

Get comfortable in bed. Take three deep breaths and consciously relax the body. Breathe in to your lower tummy so it rises first, and then full up the mid chest so it rises secondly, then lastly, breath into upper chest. In other words a full deep breathe. Hold your breath to count of a three full seconds then slowly exhale fully. Repeat this two more times. You then mentally focus and place your awareness into your toes and notice all the feelings your toes can feel. Once you have noticed and ticked off all the feeling you are aware of in your toes move onto all the feelings your <u>feet</u> are registering. Next you move your awareness to your <u>shins and calves</u>.

Next more your awareness to your <u>thighs</u> and see what you can feel. Next move your awareness to your <u>buttocks,</u> see what they are feeling.

Next become aware of your <u>hips</u>, what are they feeling? Then your <u>lower back,</u> what is that feeling? Now be aware of your <u>tummy</u> and all it feels. Now be aware of your <u>upper back</u>. Next is <u>chest</u> what can you feel? Next be aware of your <u>shoulders</u>. Now become aware of your <u>fingers and hands</u>. Next become aware of <u>forearms</u>. Now go on to your <u>upper arms</u> imagine the relaxation now felt in your hands and arms, joining the relaxation experienced in the body and shoulders. Now shift your awareness to your <u>neck muscles</u>. Now be aware of the <u>scalp</u> and let that relax and then finally the <u>facial muscles</u> let them relax in the same way, being aware of any feelings experienced.

Chances are you will be asleep before finishing the exercise. If you find your mind wondering onto other things, gently drift back to it and start relaxation again. <u>There are three aspects to sleep</u> Firstly: - It is the time when the body is able to relax and rejuvenate itself. Sleep also provides the ideal opportunity for the body to cleanse itself internally and replace damaged cells.

Secondly: - It is vital that when you sleep, you sleep in total darkness. Try not to even have a light from a digital clock shining on you, in the room. Have good curtains to block out any light from the street. The sleep we have between 11:00pm and 6:00am is particularly important. Only during this period of time and only if in complete darkness the brain releases "melatonin." Test results have linked melatonin with the ability to kill cancer cells.

Thirdly: - It is also when you sleep that your soul leaves your body as it were, and carries out work on other planes. Your soul goes over the lessons of the day, and sets up the lessons for the coming day. You communicate with your guardian angels and higher spirits and recharge on spirit energy. Emotional problems from the day can be resolved while we sleep. There is a saying “Sleep Restoreth My Soul” I don’t know who said that, but whoever it was, knew a thing or two. This is why a good 7 – 8 hours of natural sleep is very important to staying young.

Other General Physical Tips.

1) Guys, if you’re heterosexual now, then, using a good **moisturising cream** on your face after shaving, won’t change your sexual orientation. Our facial skin is probably the only part of our bodies that is almost always exposed to weather and the elements. I use a product called “Bio-oil” at time of writing, but ask some woman friends for their recommendations.. Don’t skimp; spend the money! You can moisturise your neck, knees, heels, elbows and all other parts of the body as well if you want, but at least do your face and neck.

2) On the subject of weather and the elements.
Sun Block is important. Excessive ultra violet rays from the sun do and will age your skin so wearing a good quality strong sun block is important for anti-aging but also to help prevent skin cancer. (Suggestion: Studies are showing how it is beneficial to experience a small amount of sunlight directly on to our skin as it forces out body to manufacture vitamin D. Vitamin D has been shown to have an anti cancer effect. The emphasis however is a small amount of direct sunlight, I would say no more than 10 minutes or so after which cover-up with sun

block. Obviously, commonsense needs to prevail and moderation and avoiding peak times of exposure during summer).

3) Why not combine some sort of activity that you enjoy or something you always thought you would like to do one day? What better time than now? Perhaps an activity or sport you used to do when younger but over the years you have "let it go" by the way side. Think of something you would like to do that involves physical exertion of some sort and to some degree. For me it is dancing. It is fun, social and energetic. What about tennis, netball, swimming, golf, fencing, bowls, squash, and hiking. The choices are endless.

Before moving onto the next section, please remember to combine all aspects of this book in a holistic way. You will find that each segment complements and enhances the beneficial effects of the other six segments. With this combination, there is a synergistic effect, so, collectively applied; they will bring dramatic changes into your life on all levels.

Nutrition

When it comes to nutrition there are even more experts than there are on the physical side of the equation. Over the years I have settled on some simple rules that work very well. I am equally sure that some 'experts' would gasp at them. We need simple rules that are easy to remember with no measuring of calories or portions or all the complicated things you can read about in diet books. The average Joe and Josephine (like me) can't be bothered with all the technical stuff. If it is not simple we won't do it, will we? So saying that, this is what I follow for Youthing and it will work for you as well.

No junk food or drink! This means: - no junk food like chocolate, biscuits, sweets, ice cream, lollies, cakes, pastries, pizza, fast foods, muffins and such like. It also means no soft drinks, fizzy drinks. As I am a lazy man and I know how weak willed I am. I have a rule that one day a week I can eat anything I want. For me it is usually either Saturday or Sunday. The reason for this is that these are the two days I will most likely go out and be social. On this day, if I want to binge out on chocolate or whatever I want, I know I can.

This means I don't feel so deprived. I also don't have to feel guilty. It makes it easier to get through the week and be disciplined with myself. After a while you will find that when you get to an "indulge" day, you may not want to indulge as much, if at all. Let this happen naturally but remember if you don't indulge on that day it is another week before you can indulge. You cannot carry it forward.

Try to make your "day of indulgence "the same one every week, instead of changing it all the time. If your goal is to lose some weight then I'm sorry but foods to avoid (except on indulge days) are: -

Potatoes

Pasta

Bread (You can have a maximum of 2 slices a day – the darker the better)

Rice

I tend to avoid foods that are high in carbohydrates and eat as much as I like of high protein content food i.e. meat, fish, cheese, eggs, etc, cooked any way you want. Make sure however to only eat the one food concentrate at a time - see notes below on food combining. Eat as much fresh fruit and salad type foods as you want, when you want. Eat six smaller meals a day. This is vital as it maintains energy levels and stops blood sugar levels from fluctuating. So eat something in the morning, mid morning, lunch, afternoon, and dinnertime and in the early evening up to 8:00 pm.

If you eat like this you won't feel as hungry and be tempted to snack on junk. Force yourself to eat in this manner even if you are not hungry. You will find it helps to stabilise your metabolism. The smaller type meals can be a couple of apples or two bananas or other fruit. The bigger meals can be a salad and steak or fish or a vegetarian dish. Have a water bottle with you and drink plenty of water – I can't stress this enough - none of us drink enough. When you think you have drunk enough – drink some more!

The following is all about combining our food to maximise our health. It outlines simple rules that are well worth memorising and applying in our lives. “Eat to live not live to Eat”. The body has a certain amount of energy at its disposal at any given point in time. This energy I like to call vital energy but it goes by many names, “chi” in Chinese philosophy, “prana” in Indian philosophy to name but two.

Vital energy comes into the body through various means; good nutrition being a biggie but also it can be enhanced by meditation, certain breathing exercises, Qigong, Yoga, having balanced chakra and exercise generally. Activities that deplete this vital energy are, stress, lack of correct sleep, pollution, inharmonious relationships, not living a life in accordance with your reason for incarnating, harbouring negative emotions, and significantly and most commonly:- bad eating habits and bad eating cycles. The single largest use of vital energy in the body, without a doubt - is used for the process of digestion.

If there is a surplus of vital energy in the body, more than the amount of energy required by the body for the digestion process, then the extra energy is automatically used by the “body intelligence” to detoxify itself, to slim down, and therefore be healthier and live longer. It follows that the more we can do to aid the process of digestion and thus use less of this vital energy then the more vital energy will be left over to combat any bacteria or virus encountered in the environment, to get rid of any toxins in the body, to eliminate fat stored on the body, to better cope with stress and to ensure good healthy sleep. These all added together mean living longer and enjoying a much healthier lifestyle.

“Here are some relatively simple rules of eating to follow to ensure you maximise your vital energy available to give you great health and a slim fitter body.” Understand the body cycles and how to eat and when to eat and what to eat. The body has three cycles of time where different activities take place at different times of the day and night.

They are as follows 1) 12:00 pm in the afternoon till 8:00 pm at night – Eating - taking in food into the body. 2) 8:00 pm till 4:00 am in the morning – assimilation of food the body is digesting and taking the nutrients from the food into the body via the intestines. 3) 4:00 am in morning till 12:00 pm in afternoon – Elimination - the body is getting ready to eject waste products from food out of the body.

In an ideal world only eating between 12:00 pm and 8:00 pm would be best but it is not an ideal world so if you have to eat breakfast or snack before 12:00 pm lunchtime limit your intake to fruit only. As much fruit as you want but only fruit. ONLY EVER EAT FRUIT ON AN EMPTY STOMACH. So that means you can eat fruit from when you wake up in the morning till 30 minutes (or 45 minutes if bananas or avocados have been eaten) before you sit down to eat a properly combined meal. Then you would have to allow 4 hours to pass before (if last meal was properly combined – will explain this concept soon) or 8 hours have passed if improperly combined meal has been eaten, before you can eat fruit again.

The reason for this is fruit takes approximately 30 minutes to leave the stomach after eating and if you have eaten bananas or avocados then you must allow 45 minutes to pass before you eat any other food. Fruit if eaten combined with any other food will stay trapped in the stomach for at least 4 to 8 hours with that other food and what happens is after 30 to 45 minutes fruit in the stomach starts to ferment. This causes bloating feeling, indigestion feelings and poor assimilation of food. This is why eating fruit should always be on an empty stomach. It means no fruit deserts after a meal as well! The fruit when eaten correctly takes virtually no body vital energy to digest and it will clean the internal body as it passes through the body and it will hydrate the body as well because of it's high water content.

Let's define what exactly is a properly combined meal. This is any meal that contains only ONE concentrated food source and as much vegetables and or salads as you wish with it. So for example – a steak and vegetables and or a salad. Lets define what is a concentrated food source. Apply this rule -- if the food is not a vegetable or a salad then it is a concentrated food. So if it is not natural out of the ground food, if it has been processed or changed in any way (apart from cooking) then it is a concentrated food. There are two notable exceptions. One is the POTATO. If it were eaten just peeled and uncooked then it would be fine it would be a pure vegetable but once it is cooked it moves over to being a concentrated food. Rice once cooked is also a concentred food by itself. Obviously therefore bread, pasta, pizza, cheese, diary products are all concentrated foods and should be eaten alone and with vegetables and or salads.

So as an example – steak and vegetables and or salads is fine and potato and vegetables and or salads are fine BUT steak and another concentrated food like "potato" with vegetables and or salads would not be fine. The reason is simple. A properly combined meal passes through the stomach in approximately 4 hours. An improperly combined meal takes 8 hours atleast. This means it uses up, twice as much vital energy to digest food. It compounds a problem because the 8 hours it takes to leave the stomach will often as not throw the three cycles of the body out of whack. So you will still be trying to digest an improperly combined meal when you have shifted into the time period when the body wants to naturally not digest any more but rather it is geared to assimilate nutrients in the intestines. This also adds a huge burden of energy use from the vital energy available.

The reason an improperly combined food takes 8 hours to pass from the stomach is as follows - using the example of a meal consisting of steak, potatoes and salad. Firstly vegetables and salads will digest in either an alkaline or acidic stomach, so that is why it doesn't matter, what singular concentrate food you eat with them. Steak however when you eat it is a protein and so the stomach secretes acid to digest the protein. However potato is a starch and so the mouth via chewing and saliva secretes alkali to digest that. This is where the problem sets in.

The acid and the alkali neutralise each other in the stomach and so digestion is severely effected, food is no longer broken down in the stomach as effectively and it takes longer to leave the stomach. Often as much as 8 hours instead of 4 hours. Also after 8 hours the stomach will pass the food on into the bowels regardless of whether or not it is fully digested. So that means the intestines now have to work even harder to break down the by then, rotting food! So you can see that by following these relatively simple rules you will free up huge amounts of vital energy that the body will automatically use to detoxify your body, to get rid of any excess weight, and give you more vitality and energy to enjoy your life. I challenge you to try it for just 21 days and see what a difference it will make to your lifestyle.

Final word on nutrition

As a final comment on nutrition I feel I have to add at this point, especially for the "spiritually minded individual" that ultimately the complete removal of all refined foods and the removal of all meat and dairy products from ones diet is the best way of achieving the best possible health – nutrition wise. So this means eliminating all meat, fish, milk, yogurt, cheese etc. from our diet and eating mainly nuts, fruit and vegetables - in effect a vegan diet.

I understand that not everyone is ready for this but any movement in this direction is beneficial, of this I am certain. I myself am moving in this direction, but at time of writing am not there yet. So much research has been done on this subject comparing countries that eat little or no meat or dairy products to those countries - mainly western countries - that eat a lot of meat and dairy products and invariably those countries have major health problems with high numbers of cancer, diabetes, obesity and heart disease to name a few.

From a spiritual point of view one must also think about the cruelty to animals that occur, in most of the farming practices carried out today as well. Does one want to contribute to that is a question only the individual can answer?

Multivitamin

Invest in a good quality multivitamin supplement and be sure to take it daily. The variety, and worse, the quantity of vegetables and fruit we need to eat each day to ensure that we receive the 'correct' amount of vitamins into our body is staggeringly large. I know what I am like. Like any good average Joe I would soon give up on any attempt to achieve what the experts say I need to do to get the correct amount. So a good multivitamin and mineral tablet a day seems commonsense to me. It is quick, easy and effective and so naturally has instant appeal.

Trace Elements and Minerals

This is something I am passionate about. What are trace elements and minerals? They are basically a collection of minute amounts of metals and minerals that the body NEEDS to work internally efficiently. The human body is a walking chemical factory. Every day millions of chemical reactions are occurring in the human body. In order for these chemical reactions to occur naturally, certain trace minerals need to be present. It stands to reason if the body is short of some elements it will not function properly.

Examples of these are: - selenium, boron, iron, zinc, manganese, copper, cobalt, sulphur and iodine, to name a few. In years past humans would obtain all the minerals they needed from the food they consumed. Plants absorb minerals from the soil, which we in turn eat and so absorb into our systems, ready for the body to utilise in its chemical reactions. In modern times in response to making more money, and thus forcing greater productivity in terms of the amount of crops produced from a given field; the soil itself has become depleted of trace elements and minerals. The problem is further compounded I believe, by the extensive use of super phosphates applied to fields to increase productivity.

Super phosphates inhibit a plant's ability to absorb trace elements from the soil and so the problem gets worse. Modern day fruit and vegetables don't contain sufficient amounts of vitamins and minerals in order to properly nourish our bodies. You only have to taste the difference between organic vegetables and non-organic vegetables to sense this. It is for this reason that a good daily supplement containing essential trace elements, vitamins and minerals, is vital for our bodies to function well, remain in excellent health, and stay young.

I personally get my supply from a company in New Zealand called Health House. Here is their website www.healthouse.co.nzwww.healthousc.co.nz. I use four of their products to cover the range I feel is important for the body, to help prevent aging and create a longer life. They are as follows: - CAA, Coral C, CQ10 with Omega 3 and two teaspoons a day of Colloidal Silver. I recommend these products or similar from your own source.

The other supplement I recommend is vitamin C because unlike animals the human body cannot manufacture it. Vitamin C helps with many body functions including the immune system, so a good regular source of this vitamin is crucial to optimum health. It is very simple really. I know that experts would tweak this and tweak that and have all sorts of suggestions for the average Joe to do or not do, but at the end of the day these simple lifestyle changes will youth your body.

Add together the five yoga techniques, the increased exercise routines covered, and nutrition in the way i have described it above, and you are well on the way to feeling younger. Again, results speak for themselves, so try it out over the next three months.

And be prepared to be amazed.

Meditation

In recent times many studies have proven the beneficial results that meditation has on the body and mind. Over most of my life I have meditated on and off and have realised the benefits of the practice. As time has past, and having started down the anti-aging track as a focus, I realised that some aspects of meditation are important to anti-aging. Numerous tests have shown that modern day stress does have a negative effect on the body. It can cause the body to become overly acidic which in turn can result in various diseases and disorders and contribute to premature aging. It has been proven that people who meditate regularly experience much less stress in their body and mind. It follows therefore, that meditation is a method of aiding Youthing.

So what is meditation?

I have already mentioned that "crust" that surrounds our core 'true essential self' and our 'higher self' and have called it our 'lower self' or ego self. This lower self is always chattering away in our minds. It is always thinking, calculating, worrying, running what-if situations, going over what happened yesterday or even years ago and wondering what might happen tomorrow etc. It is like a monkey jumping from tree-to-tree or thought-to-thought.

It is that part, which at night, when we are trying to sleep, keeps leaping about from thought to thought, often without any real direction. It talks so much, makes so much noise that we can't hear the "still small voice" within, which is our higher self and the inner core God part. Meditation is a technique to still that chatterbox and place us into a meditative and or contemplative state where we can listen to the deeper knowledge that is inside all of us. All this is in addition to the health benefits to the body itself.

The basic procedure of meditation is as follows: Collect your conscious mind and give it something to focus on solely. You can use different techniques to suit your circumstances and personal preference. For example, a candle flame in front of you, a word that has no meaning attached to it i.e. "Iyim" repeated over and over again in your mind's eye, or picture in vivid detail some beautiful scenery that you create and can explore mentally.

Having decided what you are going to use to focus on, you first sit comfortably upright. Not laying down as then you may have a tendency to fall asleep. Very quickly you relax the body as I have already shown you. This time however you go through the relaxation exercise relatively quickly no more than five minutes. Again I repeat it here as a reminder and to save you looking back. Take <u>three deep breaths</u> and consciously relax the body. Breathe in to your lower tummy so it rises first, and then full up the mid chest so it rises secondly, then lastly, breath into upper chest. In other words a full deep breathe.

Hold your breath to count of a three full seconds then slowly exhale fully. Repeat this two more times. You then mentally focus and place your awareness into your <u>toes</u> and notice all the feelings your toes can feel. Once you have noticed and ticked off all the feeling you are aware of in your toes, move onto all the feelings your <u>feet</u> are registering. Next you move your awareness to your <u>shins and calves</u>. Next more your awareness to your <u>thighs</u> and see what you can feel. Next move your awareness to your <u>buttocks</u> see what they are feeling. Next become aware of your <u>hips</u>, what are they feeling? Then your <u>lower back</u> what is that feeling? Now be aware of your <u>tummy</u> and all it feels. Now be aware of your <u>upper back</u>. Next is <u>chest</u> what can you feel? Next be aware of your <u>shoulders</u>. Now become aware of your <u>fingers and hands</u>. Next become aware of <u>forearms</u>.

Now go on to your upper arms, imagine the relaxation now felt in your hands and arms, joining the relaxation experienced in the body and shoulders. Now shift your awareness to your neck muscles. Now be aware of the scalp and let it relax and then finally the facial muscles, let them relax in the same way, being aware of any feelings experienced. Once your body is feeling more relaxed and you are breathing normally, you then focus all your attention onto your word without meaning, or your candle or visualization.

Your goal is to do this focusing for 20 minutes once a day. Those who want to can do it 20 minutes in morning and again 20 minutes at night. One 20-minute session per day, is enough for the average lazy man like me however.

The unexplained secret of meditation: A lot of people have tried meditation, (perhaps you yourself have in the past) and they have given up on it. They have had all sorts of wonderful and weird expectations about it, gleaned I suspect from the Hollywood version of some Chinese Kung Fu expert who becomes mysteriously enlightened and when nothing happens like that, they give it up as a bad joke. They haven't understood the unexplained secret of meditation. A secret, so simple, that it appears as nothing.

What people don't understand about meditation is that as you meditate your mind will wonder off the subject of your focus i.e. the candle, the word or beautiful scenery. It is normal, natural and bound to happen. One moment you're repeating the word "Iyim" then next minute you realise that for the last 3-4 minutes you have been thinking about the dishes that need doing, or the lawns that need mowing or the tasks you have to do at work tomorrow. In other words you suddenly notice you have drifted away from your focus point. This is where most people get annoyed with themselves, or get frustrated and think they are doing it wrong. They often give it up and say "it doesn't work for me."

As I have said, this is perfectly normal. What you do, when this drifting occurs, is without rebuking yourself, gently return your mind to the focus of your awareness, until the 20 minutes has past. The secret is that every time you notice you have drifted away from your chosen focus, you quietly refocus on the candle, the word, or scenery: your body has also just relaxed a notch.

You see, as we experience things in our day-to-day life, i.e. little traumas of the day at work, any stress experienced, be it emotional or physical and no matter how slight: our muscles tense and remember these incidents. When you drift away from the focus point to some random thought it means your body muscles are giving up the stress stored in them. I know this sounds weird but none the less it is true. So you see, rather than rebuke yourself for not being able to meditate correctly you should be happy that you are in fact doing very well and actually de-stressing yourself and in that process aiding your body to youth itself.

Another benefit of meditation for the spiritually inclined; After a period of time and practice at stilling the mind chatter, the lower self falls away and you are able to open yourself to direct communication with the essential self via your higher self. You may experience moments of inspiration ranging from the mundane i.e. a solution to a problem you have, springing spontaneously into your mind; to the sublime feeling of connectivity with the wholeness of life itself. In between are experiences ranging from feeling centered and stronger within yourself, to hearing your guides talking with you as clearly as you can talk to a friend over a coffee.

You can learn things directly from them on how the world actually works and how things are. You can learn to see them and learn their names. You will find more and more little 'miracles' happening in your life and every day is looked forward to as an exciting adventure.

Insights may come, as to what your original purpose was for incarnating into this lifetime and ways to bring into manifestation your divine purpose that only you can fulfil this time around. It truly is exciting when you live your life in accordance with your divine design. Reports from scientists who have been studying the brains of people who have been meditating for 20 years or more, show they have found the brains of meditators have altered slightly. They have literally grown new neural pathways connecting the left and right hemispheres of the brain. .

Science has proved that an accident-damaged brain can change and grow and some people can, over time, recover and use of parts of their body, which were previously paralysed. The brain has adapted to the injury and as a result other parts of the brain have taken over their functions. If it can do this, then it is not hard to believe that new neural pathways can be forged and connected.

Recently I have come across modern ways of inducing a meditative state using sound waves and special frequencies, which make it possible to achieve the same results in one year that would normally require up to twenty years of meditation. You may wish to investigate this methodology and apply it. See sites below for more information:

www.meditate.com.au

www.centrepointe.com

"Way of the Inner Warrior"
How emotional suppression ages us

I debated long and hard with myself as to whether I should include this section in the book. On the one hand, I know how important not suppressing ourselves emotionally is to anti-aging. On the other hand, of all the sections I realise how hard it will be to convey in the written word the techniques I use to resolve emotional repression and gain health and youth. I also realised it could be the most controversial aspect of this book.

I know from personal experience that one of the hardest things for a person to do is look within themselves, to root out inner demons as it were, inner fears and emotionally face up to the choices we make in our lives. However I decided finally that to omit this section would deprive those who could gain benefit from its inclusion. Using this section and the techniques taught can be life changing.

So let us begin. We are human beings. Human beings experience emotions. Emotions can range from beautiful feelings of love and joy to obsessive thoughts and feelings of dark depression. Emotions affect the body just as the body affects the emotions. Uplifting emotions like love, hope, passion, laughter, excitement, etc. bring joy to the body. When we experience these feelings the body releases endorphins and hormones that heal and 'youth' the body.

Conversely, dark emotions such as fear, worry, envy, jealousy, bitterness, anger, hatred, also affect the body, unfortunately, negatively. If experienced for prolonged periods of time they age us. They cause the body to experience disease, (dis-ease) which often leads to ill health and even ultimately death of the body. Uplifting emotions we should encourage and enjoy, as they will keep us young, alive and vital. Any dark emotions that we suppress, and don't face up to, go on to cause more problems, in our lives. This is to be avoided at all times as they can literally kill us or at the very least, age us. I learnt many years ago that no one survives childhood on some level at least, without being neurotic. It is true that some of us are affected to a greater or lesser degree but none the less we are all still neurotic in some areas of our lives. It can also be said that some of us have learnt to hide the effects better than others.

It is also true that subsequent life experience can negate or mitigate the original negative experiences as well. However the fact remains on some level and to some degree the average Joe and Josephine is a walking bag of neuroses. I can hear someone saying "Oh no, I disagree, I had perfect parents and a trauma free childhood, and so I don't suppress emotions or have any unresolved issues."

Well guess again. You're human, you're still incarnated in a human body, and so you still have lessons to learn. The reality is, in my opinion, the natural state for a fully integrated human being is to feel a sense of balance inside, an inner joy and harmony, to be healthy in body, to sleep easily and well with pleasant dreams, to have fulfilling relationships, work we enjoy and enough money to achieve what is important in our life. It is also important to have a sense of purpose in life, to experience daily miracles of one kind or another and to experience fulfilment when we help others.

If we are not experiencing these feelings then somewhere, on some level, we have strayed from our soul path in life and that straying has occurred because we suppressed a part of ourselves from expressing itself. Any suppression has a negative effect on our body and can manifest ill health, aging and even death, if prolonged in nature.

I will give three examples from my own life where suppression of emotions, avoidance of expressing feelings, avoiding making tough decisions and living a "not a true to myself" life had damaging effects.

Example One

I was about 33 years old. I was running a sales meeting. Suddenly I felt the right side of my face go numb and lose mobility. I finished the sales meeting and the rest of the day at work. That night I thought I had better go to the hospital for a checkup in case I had experienced a mild stroke. After undergoing tests, it turned out I had "Bells Palsy." I was told a virus causes it, attacking the sheath of the nerves, which feed and control the muscles of the face. In this case the right side of my face. Doctors talked of taking steroids to fix it and I was told it could take a few weeks and up to a year to recover. At that point I had two choices. Accept that this is the way it was and wait and hope it cures itself over time or ...

Understanding spirituality, I realised I had to have created this for a reason. There was a lesson in this illness for me to learn from. I knew that because it had occurred I must have been suppressing emotions and avoiding and not resolving issues going on for me at that point in my life. The first thing I will say is accepting that I was the cause of this illness took a certain amount of self-analysis. It always takes courage to look within. It takes complete honesty with yourself. It takes "soul searching". (Note those words well).

What I did know back then was that to have a physical illness was a symptom of an emotional or spiritual imbalance. I also know that usually for me, (and this does vary from person to person), there are usually at least five areas of conflicts I had been avoiding facing up to and dealing with in my life. So I sat down for one hour. I had a pen and paper handy. Firstly I relaxed myself in the manner I have already described in the book. I then meditated for 20 minutes to centre myself and slow down the "mind chatter' and to get into a mind space where I could listen to my inner voice as it were. I took the paper and wrote on it "Why having Bells Palsy now is good for me and what does it mean I can avoid?" Now think about that for a moment. How can anyone in their right mind even consider that there are benefits to having any illness! Well guess what? – There can be!

So I started to write down anything that came into my mind no matter how strange or bizarre they may have been, and with complete honesty. It didn't matter how embarrassing they were, no matter how 'off the wall' they seemed, without judging them or myself. This is important element when looking within. It turns out there were 15 perfectly good reasons to have Bells Palsy!

I can't remember them all now but some of them I do remember were: -

1) I was married at the time in a relationship I was not happy in. I wasn't facing (notice that word facing) up to these unhappy feelings. Easier to have an expressionless face i.e. Bells Palsy, to mirror the fact I wasn't expressing myself.
2) The Bells Palsy got me sympathy from people
3) I had been working very hard with no break for six months so it could force me to take a rest.
4) I was booked to go to Perth in Australia for a conference to run a workshop that I didn't really want to do. The Bells Palsy was the perfect excuse as the "powers that be" couldn't make a 'poor' person suffering from such an illness go.

5) At the time I felt numb inside and it finally expressed itself as numbness in my face!

You get the point. In fact there were 10 other reasons for having the Bells palsy but as I say, usually five or more is enough for me to be triggered either to have a physical illness of some kind OR an accident where I hurt myself.

Yes even ‘accidents’ that seem not of my making, can be a sign of being out of balance either emotionally or spiritually. I then re-read and studied the reasons. Then I set about making a plan to resolve the issues. In other words, the conflicts, worries and stresses I was vaguely aware I had been pushing aside, not dealing with. They had only gone underground, as they never go away. This is another important thing to remember. They never go away, they go into the subconscious, which then tries to work out ways for you to cope with them. Often as not, ill health is one way it achieves this goal.

In this case I immediately booked a holiday and dealt with the relationship issues head on. I did do the workshop still but my subconscious knew a holiday wasn’t far behind the conference date and seemed satisfied with that arrangement. Almost immediately there was an improvement in the Bells Palsy and within two days I was back to normal, all without any treatment from doctors.

An important thing to remember is once you do decide on a course of action to eliminate a problem, you must carry it through. Don’t fall into the trap, when you start to feel better, of betraying your subconscious mind and not carrying out your resolution. The subconscious will just re-manifest the problem or a different one, possibly worse, to achieve the same result.

Example two

I was about 27 years old. I was moving apartments. When you move the last task you do is cleaning. So there I was cleaning, cleaning and cleaning. At the time I was quite directionless in my life or more correctly I was avoiding making some big decisions for my life. I had finished cleaning the top part of the stove and was bending down, head in oven part cleaning that part of the stove.

Meantime unbeknown to me while I had been cleaning the top part of the stove where the elements are, I had inadvertently turned the front element onto full. The element was one of those spiral ones as opposed to a flat element. Anyway you can guess what happened, after finishing the oven part I reached up with my left hand to the top of the stove to lever myself up. My hand clasped straight onto the red-hot element, as I stood up I saw what had happened, the burn was so bad I didn't register the pain immediately. I pulled my hand away noticing that it stuck to the element but I just had to get it off, which I did eventually.

I immediately turned on the cold water and plunged my hand into the stream. I knew while standing there I was in serious trouble. Immediately I thought back to what exactly I had been thinking about whilst I was cleaning the oven. I realised that I was thinking about my conflicts, without really knowing it. I had been going over them, almost below my conscious level as I was cleaning. With my hand under the tap water I there and then decided exactly what direction I was going to go in my life and made decisions that I had been putting off.

Hard though it is to believe, after a further 10 minutes of cold water, I pulled my hand out of the water. No pain, no scars, completely normal. This is another example of how powerful the inner self truly is.

Example three

This last example, involves a friend of mine. I was 30 years old at the time. My friend would have been about 27 years old. At the time I owned a 100-acre hobby farm in the far North of the North Island of New Zealand. It was a ramshackle place with a very old farmhouse on it. We were out in one of the fields doing some scrub cutting; I was facing in one direction, when behind me I heard a scream of pain. I turned around in time to see my friend pulling the edge of his axe out of his shin. I remember an inch of white bone exposed before the blood started coving it. He had sat down by the time I got to him and I pushed the skin together and held it in place. Fortunately he was quite a spiritual guy as well, so I said to him, "Think back to what you were thinking about just prior to getting hit by the axe." He proceeded to tell me about a conflict he had with his girlfriend at the time. We chatted for about ten minutes all around different aspects of this subject. I helped him back to the farmhouse. The farm was miles out in the country so I got some clear tape and wrapped it around his leg making sure the cut skin jaws pulled together.

We then discussed for an hour all his conflicts again and I helped him to come to decisions as to what action he was going to take to resolve them, when we got back into civilization. Short story, next day when he woke up, we took the tape of his leg, the wound was completely healed, no scars, it was as if it never happened. I will come back to these three examples soon.

<u>Recapping the steps to take if you are manifesting an illness or have accidents or experiencing some disharmonious life situation:</u>

1) Put aside at least one full hour of time where you will be uninterrupted.
2) Have pen and paper at the ready.
3) On each sheet of paper write the list of questions below. One per page. These questions can help jog your mind into looking into the right areas for where the problems might be.
4) Firstly relax the body as already described in book previously
5) Meditate to quieten the mind chatter for 20 minutes.
6) Take the pen and paper and go to the first question. Think about it and take your time. Write anything down that comes to mind no matter how weird, silly, funny, embarrassing, painful, and hurtful it may be. Don't judge yourself. We are human and so, we are all "weirdo's" really. There are usually at least five different conflicts or areas of stress if something has manifested as an illness / accident / situation in my life.
7) Work through the next question and so on, remembering they can overlap, so one set of answers may cover all the questions or a few of them.
8) THEN work out and decide then and there on a course of ACTION you WILL take to resolve the conflicts. You must take these actions for failure to do so means the subconscious will maintain the status quo. Forewarned is forearmed.
9) Once you have finished take three deep breaths
10) Go forward to place into action all the decisions you have come to.

Questions (One per page)

- What are the benefits to me having this illness / accident / situation in my life?
- What does it stop me doing?
- What does it mean I have to do differently because of it?
- What conflicts do I have right now in my life that are affected either positively or negatively because of this illness / accident / situation in my life?
- What am I avoiding in my life right now? How does it relate to this illness / accident / situation in my life?
- If I had to name one conflict I am avoiding facing up to, or making a decision about, what would that be?
- By having this illness / accident / situation in my life what don't I have to face up to in my life?
- By having this illness / accident / situation in my life what does it force me to face up to?

You can see from the three examples from my life that suppression and avoidance of conflicts, not living a life true to your essential inner self, can manifest not only ill health but also can cause "accidents", and draw unfavourable life situations or even unsavoury people into your life. It can lead to being in the wrong place at the wrong time; for you are out of step with your intuitive self. Remember your intuition, your inner-tuition, is the faculty by which your higher God-self communicates to your lower ego self.

Emotional suppression and avoidance in resolving conflicts is from your lower self, your ego self and when that happens you cut yourself off from your higher self and the miracles it can bring into your life including anti-aging. There is no doubt in my mind that the answers do lie within us and this introspective approach is the best way to ensure that the lower self has less of an influence and the higher self becomes more involved in our daily affairs.

There are times however when we encounter some stressful situation or experience when we just don't have time or the circumstances As a STOP GAP measure until you find the time later on to do the introspective technique properly I have three pieces of advice that have carried me through some bad times. I call these band-aids.

They are as follows: -

1) It has been said, that at least 80% of all things we worry about never ever happen. So why worry? Remind yourself of this fact next time you find yourself worrying.
2) When confronted with any negative situation I ask myself the following question to gain perspective. "Will this really matter to me in five years time?" Not many things that get you upset or uptight now, will actually affect you in five years. So why let them now?
3) I say "This too will pass." Everything changes including negative or bad situations so reminding yourself that everything passes is a good idea to gain some perspective.

This now brings me to explain the title of this chapter.

"The Way of the Inward Warrior"

I have mentioned it before and will again now. The more we recognise and accept this concept the sooner and faster it will manifest in our lives. Inside all of us is our essential self. It is our God/ Goddess self. It is that part of ourselves that connects us to the essence of everything. It is that part of us that feels connected with life. It is the part of ourselves that can be allowed to come forward by listening to it, by stilling that 'chatter mind' of the lower self, the ego self.

It is this part that gives us our intuition, meaning, inner-tuition. By listening to it and living our lives by its promptings, we connect with a wellspring of energy and life force. By doing so, we will add years to our life and life to our years. This is the path of the inner warrior. This is the road less travelled. We need to become aware with total self honesty when we are acting out of our lower ego selves and choose to put aside these reactions, and via our higher selves allow the inner essential core-self to have its way.

This has been called surrendering to God.

I call it surrendering to the God/Goddess within. Miracles happen daily in our lives when we "Let go and Let God.

Characteristics of lower self, ego realities are:-

1) It almost always serves self-interest first and foremost.
2) It is often win/lose scenarios.
3) It is controlling.
4) It involves activities, schemes and manipulations where the end result, if not achieved, brings feelings of loss of face or loss of self-esteem.
5) It can lead to ill health, accidents, disharmonious situations or dealing with negative people in our lives.
6) Rapid aging.

Characteristics of higher self realities are:

1) Life is effortless.
2) Miracles happen daily.
3) Opportunities just spring out at you with no real effort.
4) Perfect youthful health abides in the body
5) Monetary needs are always taken care of to achieve a "higher-self" goal - note well, I said, a "higher self" goal.
6) You find yourself always in the right place at the right time.
7) You have selfless goals, behaviours and activities that benefit everyone involved.
8) They manifest in joyous feelings inside and you have perfect work, great relationships and harmony in your worldly affairs.

It has been said in order to know God you have to die and be reborn. The "you" underlined means the lower ego self has to die and you have to bring forward and operate and conduct your affairs out of the essence, the God within. Effectively be "re-born." The ego lower self hates "Faith," for faith to the lower self is illogical. It means giving up control, it means it ceases to hold centre court and like all prima donnas it loves the limelight. It will fiercely resist at first. The higher self calls for active faith. Faith that when you learn to "let go and let God" the 'right' things, people and circumstances, come into your life, often in seemingly miraculous ways; but they are not miraculous at all. They are our birthright and are perfectly natural occurrences.

There is a saying, "When you know what the magician knows it is not magic". In the same way, once you tap into your higher self and let it manifest in your life, and trust and act on its inner promptings and guidance, then miracles no longer seem miraculous, as they become every day occurrences.

This is The Way of The Inner Warrior

In Summary

I have outlined the seven sections as a blueprint for a longer and more vital life.

They work.

Doing any aspect well, with regularity, will enhance your life. Doing ALL aspects, will dramatically change your life more than you can imagine, in ways you cannot imagine. Though I have tried to make the concepts as simple as possible, it will still take effort and determination to do them regularly and religiously.

The reward of Youthing is well worth making the changes, and adopting the disciplines, discussed in this book. The rewards gained by following the principles I have outlined, are so much more than the effort required achieving them. You will find that doing them makes so much sense.

I challenge you to commit to following these disciplines fully and totally for just three months.

See it as an experiment for three months. At the end of three months YOU be the judge.

I wish you a long life, vitality and all your true hearts desires. From one average Joe pilgrim to another average Joe pilgrim on the way up the mountain!

www.ingramcontent.com/pod-product-compliance
Ingram Content Group UK Ltd.
Pitfield, Milton Keynes, MK11 3LW, UK
UKHW020126250726
13967UKWH00002B/505